The Regional Dimension
of Transformation in Central Europe

Regional Policy and Development Series

Published with the Regional Studies Association

In the face of rapidly growing regional consciousness, this series tackles a wide range of important and policy relevant issues, drawing upon a strong theoretical and practical base. It makes widely available the results of work in this field and will inform and assist professionals, academics, policy makers and students with the choices that they face and the work they must undertake.

An Enlarged Europe
Regions in Competition?
*Edited by Sally Hardy, Mark Hart, Louis Albrechts
and Anastasios Katos*
ISBN 1 85302 188 1
Regional Policy and Development Series 6

The Regional Imperative
Regional Planning and Governance in Britain,
Europe and the United States
Urlan A Wannop
ISBN 1 85302 292 6
Regional Policy and Development Series 9

Regional Development Strategies
A European Perspective
Edited by Jeremy Alden and Philip Boland
ISBN 1 85302 356 6
Regional Policy and Development Series 15

Regional Policy in Europe
S.S. Artobolevskiy
ISBN 1 85302 308 6
Regional Policy and Development Series 11

Sustainable Cities
Graham Haughton and Colin Hunter
ISBN 1 85302 234 9
Regional Policy and Development Series 7

The Regional Dimension of Transformation in Central Europe

Grzegorz Gorzelak

Regional Policy and Development 10

Jessica Kingsley Publishers	Regional Studies Association
London and Bristol, Pennsylvania	London

First published in the United Kingdom in 1996 by
Jessica Kingsley Publishers Ltd
116 Pentonville Road
London N1 9JB, England
and
1900 Frost Road, Suite 101
Bristol, PA 19007, U S A
and
Regional Studies Association (Registered Charity 252269)

Copyright © 1996 Grzegorz Gorzelak

Library of Congress Cataloging in Publication Data
Gorzelak, Grzegorz.
The regional dimension of transformation in Central Europe /
Grzegorz Gorzelak.
p.   cm. -- (Regional policy and development series : 10)
Includes bibliographical references and index.
ISBN 1-85302-301-9 (pbk.)
1. Europe, Central--Economic conditions--Regional disparities,
2. Poland--Economic conditions--1990- 3. Regional planning--Europe.
Central. 4. Regional planning--Poland. I. Title. II. Series.
HC244.G624 1995
338.947--dc20   95-14819
                                                           CIP

British Library Cataloguing in Publication Data
Gorzelak, Grzegorz
Regional Dimension of Transformation in
Central Europe. - (Regional Policy &
Development Series; Vol.10)
I. Title II. Series
330.9438

ISBN 1-85302-301-9

Printed and Bound in Great Britain by
Cromwell Press. Melksham, Wiltshire

Contents

Introduction 1

Chapter 1. The General Processes of Transformation – An Overview 5

General course of Central European reforms 5
Foreign investment and foreign trade 10
Structural changes 17
Industrial restructuring 19
Privatisation 22
The labour market 27
Social costs 29
The transformation of Central Europe: a prospective view 31
Post-Fordism or Post-Communism? 32

Chapter 2. The Historic Heritage of Socio-Economic Space 35

The origins 35
The spatial economic patterns 38
Social, ethnic and political spatial patterns 42
Territorial organisation 44

Chapter 3. The Regional Patterns of Transformation 47

Demography 49
The regional product 58
The labour market 60
Economic restructuring 77
Privatisation 83
Foreign capital and new international setting 86
Regional structure of economic power 98
Transport links with Europe 101
Natural environment 106
The political profiles of Polish regions 113

**Chapter 4. The Regional Potential
for Transformation   119**

Chapter 5. Regional Policies   131
Lack of national regional policies 131
Policies of regions 135
The role of local government in local development 136
Reform of the territorial organisation of the state 139
For new approaches to regional policies in Central Europe   143

Index   149

List of Tables

1.1 GDP level compared to the European Community in 1992   5

1.2 Dynamics of basic economic categories, Poland, 1989–1993, previous
year = 100   7

1.3 Economic development of Central European countries, 1992–2005   9

1.4 Inflow of foreign capital to Poland by country of origin, 1991–1993
(estimate)   12

1.5 Major foreign investment made in Poland in 1992   14

1.6 Geographical structure of Polish exports, current prices, in percentages   15

1.7 Exports structure by main foreign markets   15

1.8 Creation of GDP in Poland, by sectors, 1989–1992   17

1.9 Structure of value added and of employment by branches in Poland, 1992   18

1.10 Sectoral structure of working in Poland, 1990–1992 (yearly averages)   18

1.11 Employment by main economic sectors, 1992–2005   19

1.12 Growth of sales in Polish industry, by branches (constant prices, the
same period of previous year = 100)   20

1.13 Growth of sales in Polish industry, by groups of activities (constant
prices, the same period of previous year = 100)   21

1.14 Employment in Polish industry, by branches, 1989–1993   22

1.15 Privatisation in Poland by type and sector, 1.08.1990–31.03.1992   25

1.16 Working in the public sphere as percentage of total number of working
in the Polish economy   25

1.17 Dynamics of the number of working in Poland, by sectors and
ownership, 1989–1991   26

1.18 Economic activity rates in Poland, 1988, 1992   27

1.19 Number of working in Poland, 1989–1993   28

1.20 Differentiation of personal incomes of employees in Poland, 1989–1991   31

2.1 Territorial and administrative structures in Central Europe   44

3.1 Arrangements of Polish voivodships according to dynamics of the
number of working, by type of ownership, 1989–1991   62

3.2 Arrangements of Polish voivodships according to dynamics of the
number of working in the private sphere, by sectors, 1989–1991   63

3.3 Economically active in Poland, by educational level, 1988   64

3.4 Academic centres in Poland and employment in science   67

3.5 Relation of registered unemployed to jobs on offer in Poland, June 1992,
by regions   73

3.6 Shares of leading Polish regions in industrial production, current prices
(1989: socialised sector only)   77

3.7 Arrangements of Polish voivodships according to labour productivity in
industry in 1991 and change of places in comparison with 1990   78

3.8 Foreign capital in Poland, 1993   87

3.9 Capitals of Central Europe as centres of location of foreign capital   92

3.10 Emission of industrial pollution in Poland   108

3.11 Pollution levels in Central Europe in 1991   109

4.1 Typology of Polish regions from the point of view of their transformation
potential   121

List of Figures

I.1   Territorial organisation of Poland (*voivodships*) — 4

1.1   GDP index for Central European countries (1989 = 100; 1993 estimates) — 7

1.2   Business cycle in Polish industry in enterprises' opinions — 8

1.3   Major imbalances in the Central European economies, 1992 — 11

1.4   Debt burden of the Central European countries — 16

1.5   The share of the private sector in GDP, 1992 — 26

1.6   Unemployment rates in Central Europe — 30

1.7   Percentage of long-term unemployed in employment — 30

2.1   Provinces of Poland, 10th–12th centuries — 36

2.2   Stability of Polish Western Border — 37

3.1   Regional differentiation of the density of population in Central Europe — 48

3.2   The biggest urban centres in Central Europe — 49

3.3   Share of population in pre-productive age in Poland, 1991 — 55

3.4   Share of population in post-productive age in Poland, 1991 — 55

3.5   Regional GDP per inhabitant in Poland in 1992 — 58

3.6   Share of agriculture in regional GDP creation in Poland in 1991 — 59

3.7   Dynamics of the number of working in the Polish economy, 1991 — 61

3.8   Percentage with university-level education in the total number of economically active in Central Europe, 1992 — 66

3.9   Academic centres in Central Europe — 69

3.10 Unemployment rates by Polish regions, April 1994 — 72

3.11 Unemployment rates in regions of Central Europe, 1992 — 74

3.12 Share of working in Polish industry in the total number of working, 1991 — 76

3.13 Privatised enterprises in the capital way and their value, June 1993 — 84

3.14 Foreign capital invested and declared to be invested in Poland, March 1993 — 87

3.15 Foreign capital invested in regions of Central Europe, 1992 — 91

3.16 Number of firms from the list of 500 biggest Polish companies, 1992 — 100

3.17 Number of employees in the firms from the list of 500 biggest companies in Poland — 100

3.18 Expected highways and traffic in Poland, 2000 — 103

3.19 Major road connections in Poland, 2000 — 104

3.20 Twenty-seven areas of endangered environment in Poland — 107

3.21 Natural environment of Central Europe — 110

3.22 Turn-out, parliamentary elections in Poland, September 1993 — 114

3.23 Votes against the course of economic reforms, parliamentary elections in Poland, September 1993 — 115

4.1   The regional potential for transformation in Poland — 122

4.2   The Central European 'boomerang' – a concentration of transformation processes — 128

5.1   Proposed new big *voivodships* in Poland — 141

Introduction

The Central European countries – in this book this term will denote the so-called 'Visegrad Group' composed of the Czech Republic, Hungary, Poland and Slovakia – entered upon the path of rapid socio-economic and political transformation only four years ago. This short period seems almost unrealistic if all changes which have already taken place are to be enumerated and the memories already fading out of the previous situation are confronted with the present-day reality of these countries.

Poland has rightly been regarded as a precursor of the evolution from 'real socialism' to (some would argue) 'unreal' capitalism in this part of the world. It adopted the most rapid and perhaps the most difficult – at least in its early stages – road to the new system. In this respect Poland might be considered as a 'laboratory of experience' of a country going through an accelerated transformation process in many dimensions: economic, political, social, environmental. Also numerous cases of delays and drawbacks of reforms, visible in Poland during the process of transformation, could be regarded as typical for other post-socialist countries.

Drawing conclusions for a wider field and making generalisations only on the basis of one example is always a dangerous endeavour. There are several differences between Poland and other Central European countries under transition: in the Czech and Slovak republics both positive and negative results of the 'velvet divorce' constitute important elements of the reality of the two new states; some claim that Hungary had begun its transformation as far back as the late 1960s, when this country introduced some relaxation to the rigid economic system of 'real socialism';[1] the Eastern European countries: Bulgaria, Rumania, post-Soviet republics seem to be in a much more difficult situation when compared with the 'Visegrad

---

1   The Hungarian reform was, to a great extent, based on the discussion of Polish economists after 1956, when the short-lived reform of the political system was introduced in Poland along with the first year of Wladyslaw Gomulka's term as the first secretary of the communist party.

Group' both in terms of material, as well as social structures and conditions. However, two arguments can be drawn in defence of using Poland as a case study:

- first, the author's access to information about and general understanding of Poland is far greater than that of any other country; the analyses may therefore be more detailed and conclusions better related to evidence than would be possible in any other case;

- second, as the results of the international project 'Eastern and Central Europe 2000' prove,[2] the mutual structural similarities of the Central European countries are so strong that the processes and phenomena of transformation – if dealt with in a general way – demonstrate more similarities than differences.

The contents of this book are rooted in the analyses conducted on the regional dimension of Poland's transformation, which were prepared for two major international projects. Three of them deserve a special mention:

- the aforementioned 'Eastern and Central Europe 2000' Project (the final report of this project was recently published by the European Commission).

- the 'Regional, Socio-Economic Development in Poland, Hungary, the Czech Republic and Slovakia', financed by the DG XVI of the CEC (Commission of the European Community) and managed by the European Policies Research Centre, University of Strathclyde;

- the set of studies and analyses carried out within the framework of the DG V-financed programme LEDA (Local Employment Development Action).

The author participated in these three projects and provided them with reports on the regional aspects of Polish and Central European transformation. These projects have resulted in rich comparative material on the regional aspects of transformation in Central Europe, which have been referred to in this analysis.

The most important question which should be posed in relation to the spatial/regional outcomes of the current transformation process and future spatial patterns of Polish – and also of other Central European countries – development is the following: *do the new factors of development follow the traditional spatial patterns of these countries or do they – and will they – change these patterns?* In other words, is the economic geography of Poland – and of other post-socialist countries of Europe

---

2   'Eastern and Central Europe 2000' (see Gorzelak *et al.* 1994) was a project financed by the DG XII of the Commission of the European Community, managed by the Institute for Human Sciences in Vienna and co-ordinated by the European Institute for Regional and Local Development, University of Warsaw. The author was the project's general co-ordinator and a co-author of its final report.

– going to change dramatically as a result of the systemic transformation, or is it going to remain, in principle, only slightly modified?

This question is derived from a reflection on the interplay between long, secular trends and current, short-term processes. As it will be briefly described in Chapter 2, the general economic spatial patterns of Polish territory have not changed throughout the centuries. This was also the case for other Central European countries, even though their political scene has been changing dramatically over the centuries. On the other hand, the emergence of major industrial centres took place only some hundred years ago, and this fact has had a deep influence on the present spatial structure of these countries (perhaps with the exception of the Czech Republic). The restructuring processes, commenced only few years ago, have already left their mark on the current spatial structures. To what extent, therefore, are these structures bound to the historical heritage and how deeply can they react to the new conditions created by the new economic and political reality?

These answers will directly lead to the regional scenario of the development of Poland within the Central European context, since superimposition of stable, historically bound spatial structures and rapid economic processes will produce the spatial structure for these countries within the next 10–15 years.

Do we – as citizens and also as those who can influence the reality – consent to these current and future patterns? If not, how should we wish to influence these processes? In this way we arrive at the problem of regional (spatial) policies and their goals.

The task of this book is to relate to all these main issues. It is structured in the following way:

1. Main economic developments of the Polish transformation are presented and related to basic processes of transformation in other post-socialist countries of Central Europe.

2. Basic features of the historic heritage of Polish socio-economic space are discussed. In particular, the spatial structure of Poland and the other three countries as inherited from the previous socialist system in 1989 is described.

3. The regional differentiation of phenomena and processes of the four-year Polish transformation are presented. Several case studies (regional and local) are recalled to illustrate this differentiation.

4. A typology of Central European regions from the point of view of their potential for adaptation to new conditions is performed. The prospected development paths of these categories are drafted, building up a scenario of regional development in Poland during the next 10–15 years.

Figure I.1 Territorial organisation of Poland (voivodships)

5. Regional policies implemented on the national and regional levels, as well as examples of local strategies, are discussed. Current reforms of the territorial organisation of the state are reported and commented upon.

6. Policy recommendations are formulated, with special stress placed on the applicability of the Western European experience to Central Europe.

References

Gorzelak, G., Kuklinski, A., Jalowiecki, B. and Zienkowski, L. (1994) 'Eastern and Central Europe 2000 – Final Report.' *Studies 2.* DGXII of the European Commission, Luxembourg.

CHAPTER 1

The General Processes
of Transformation – An Overview

General Course of Central European Reforms

The post-socialist countries of Central Europe have begun their economic, political and social transformation with a heavy burden of socialist heritage. This heritage was not entirely of a negative character. Obsolete production structures, relatively underdeveloped technical infrastructure, low level of technological, organisational and managerial advancement, and closeness of economies could be mentioned as the most important negative features. However, these countries have demonstrated a relatively well educated – though to a great extent demoralised – labour force, a higher level of social security and development of social infrastructure than could have been ascertained only from the 'pure' level of economic development.

In any case, in comparison with the West the Central European countries occupy the lowest positions (see Table 1.1). The economic reforms which were

Table 1.1 GDP level compared to
the European Community in 1992

	Czech Republic	Hungary	Poland	Slovak Republic	EC average
GDP per capita in $[a] purchasing power parity	6867	5650	5065	5320	18,518
Index: CEC = 100	125.6	103.3	92.6	97.3	338.7
Index: EC = 100	37.1	30.5	27.4	28.7	100.0
Personal consumption per capita in $ (PPP)	3743	3910	3054	2719	11,408
Index: CEC = 100	114.3	119.4	93.3	83.0	348.4
Index: EC = 100	32.8	34.3	26.8	23.8	100.0
Exchange rate as % of purchasing power	36.9	60.7	43.0	35.2	–

Note: [a] the numbers presented in the table are estimated by each country on the basis of the 1990 ICP comparisons; preliminary direct results of the ICP 1992 are the following: Czech Republic $7925, Hungary $6685, Poland $4710, Slovakia $5850.

Source: Gorzelak *et al.* (1994) Table 8.

5

introduced in these countries assumed different models of development. In Poland changes in the national economy implemented since January 1990 followed the pattern of a *shock therapy*, which resulted in deep recession and breakdown of several branches of the Polish economy. In fact, it was only very recently that the first signs of its positive effects could be seen.

Poland was unique in this respect among other post-socialist countries. As specified in the economic part of the report on the future of Central Europe (Gorzelak *et al.* 1994):

> Various approaches were chosen, ranging from the Polish 'Big bang' approach (a drastic anti-inflationary program combined with a fast liberalisation of the economy) through less radical and more pragmatic former Czechoslovak program until the most cautious Hungarian macroeconomic policy of a 'soft landing' in capitalism. Such a choice was also due to differences in the starting point for the reforms: Poland, with its hyperinflation and huge macroeconomic imbalances was not able to choose a slower, but less risky Hungarian or Czech road. A different situation occurred in the approach to privatisation. This time it was Czechoslovakia (and then the Czech and Slovak Republics) that was forced to choose the most radical, but also the most risky 'Big bang' (the voucher privatisation). Poland and Hungary, with their rapidly expanding private sectors and relatively well developing capital markets were able to introduce much more deliberate policies. In Hungary the application of the 'Big Bang' approach would not have been justified, since the transition was prepared in many respects and inflation was held under control.
>
> The problems that all the countries had to face also depended on their relative starting points. However, in spite of initial views, a strong likeness emerged in the pattern of economic problems being experienced. All the CEC economies have suffered a major drop in levels of output (in the state-owned sector), growing unemployment, and strong inflationary pressures. The collapse of the COMECON trade has led to a dramatic decrease in their exports to the Eastern markets.

During 1992, almost all of a sudden, Poland assumed the role of a leader in economic transformation among European post-socialist countries. This was due to several positive processes and phenomena, explored in more detail in the sections below. Being the first country to take the transformation path, Poland was also the first to pay economic and social costs incurred as a result of this process. However, Poland was also the first to show signs of economic recovery. 1992 was the first year which did not bring further decline of overall economic output and the increase of the GDP reached 2.2 per cent, rising to 4.5 in 1993 and to 5% in 1994. In this respect Poland appeared to be unique among all other post-socialist countries. Figures 1.1 and 1.2 present the comparison of economic performance of the post-socialist countries during the 1990s.

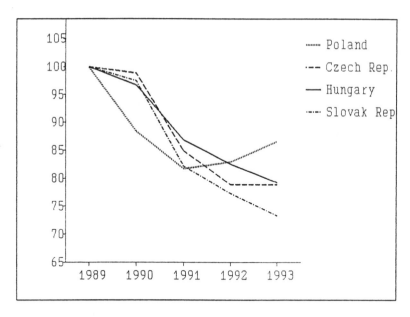

Figure 1.1 GDP index for Central European countries (1989=100)

Table 1.2 presents the dynamics of major economic categories in Poland during the transformation period.

Table 1.2 Dynamics of basic economic categories,
Poland, 1989–1993, previous year = 100

Categories	1989	1990	1991	1992	1993	1994
Gross Domestic Product	100.2	88.4	92.4	102.2	104.4	105.0
Industrial production	97.9	77.9	82.9	104.0	105.6	111.9
Agricultural production	100.9	99.7	106.8	87.2	101.5	–
Fixed capital formation	97.6	89.9	95.9	100.7	102.2	107.1
Consumption	104.9	84.6	98.6	105.0	105.0	–
Exports	100.2	113.7	97.6	97.4	113.5	118.3
Imports	101.5	82.1	137.8	113.9	115.8	113.4
Foreign investment	–	–	185.0[a]	135.0[a]	114.3	–
Working population, total	99.0	93.8	96.3	97.7	95.7	101.1
Working population, public sector	–	88.9	85.5	93.7	91.7	96.1
Working population, private sector	–	99.4	107.0	100.9	103.5	104.6
Inflation	332.0	586.0	170.3	143.0	137.6	132.0[a]

Note: a) rough estimate – no precise data available

Dynamics of industrial production of Poland in 1992 presented an upward trend since March/April. This trend was reflected in an overall growth of industrial production in 1992 and then accelerated growth in 1993 (to reach 107.4% of the 1992 level), further prolonged during the first months of 1994, when industrial production grew by more than 10 per cent in relation to the same period in 1993. However, by the end of 1993 industrial production reached only 75 per cent of the 1989 level, which shows the depth of the recession as measured by official statistics (it should be assumed that real recession was smaller, since the 'grey economy' grew substantially after 1990).

The housing sector is in an especially dramatic situation. 1993 was the 15th consecutive year of decline in the number of newly constructed dwellings, dropping in 1993 to 65 per cent of the 1992 level. In general, the number of dwellings completed has fallen to mid-1950s levels. On the other hand, the output of the entire construction sector is consistently rising, demonstrating an upward drive in capital investment.

Figure 1.2 presents evaluations of enterprises of their overall performance (replies received from 1240 industrial enterprises accounting for 22% of total industrial employment). They are systematically asked about the dynamics of their production. Since mid-1991 the upward trend is clearly visible, though as late as the end of 1993 there were more enterprises which noted growth in production than were still on a downward curve. More in-depth analyses reveal that the firms

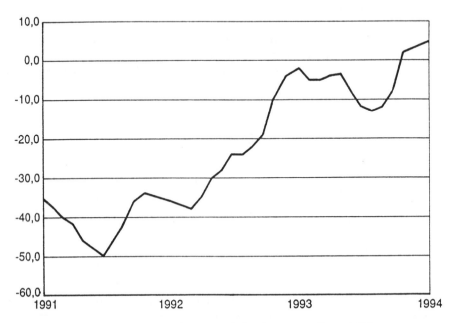

Source: Instytut Rozwoju Gospodarvego, Szkola Glowna Haudlowa 1993

Figure 1.2 Business cycle in Polish industry in enterprises' opinions

which operate in more dynamic branches are evaluating their situation as improving. A more 'optimistic' outlook is also presented by bigger enterprises, which is an interesting observation, contradicting generally held beliefs on the low effectiveness of state-owned giants (this may be, however, influenced by the relatively stronger position of big enterprises and some indirect support of the state).

In general terms, the other three Central European countries are beginning to demonstrate the first signs of recovery too. For example, in Hungary during the second quarter of 1993, industrial production reached positive dynamics (growth at the rate of 5% compared to the same period in 1992). In 1993 the GDP fell in Hungary by only -1 per cent and in 1994 it grew by 2 per cent. However, stable positive growth of the entire economy is envisaged as late as 1997. The Czech economy is recording similar results (decline of the GDP only 0.5% in 1993 and growth of 3% in 1994). In Slovakia the situation is rather more complex, since in 1993 this country had the greatest (among the four countries) decline of the GDP, equal to -4.7 per cent and also in 1994 this category fell by 2 per cent. 1995 ought to be the first year when the further decline of the Slovak economy is halted.

Table 1.3 Economic development of Central European countries, 1992–2005

Categories	Czech Republic	Hungary	Poland	Slov-akia
GDP/inhabitant, 2005 (PPP, USD of 1992)	9463	8809	8510	8505
2005/1992 GDP rate of growth, yearly average	2.5	3.4	4.5	4.1
2005/1992 personal consumption rate of growth, yearly average	2.4	3.0	4.4	3.7
2005/1992 capital formation rate of growth, yearly average	3.2	6.5	8.7	4.0
Share of gross capital formation in GDP, 2005	31.7	29.8	32.2	27.6
Net foreign investment as % of gross capital formation, 2005	6.4	9.0	9.3	13.3
Share of manufacturing in total employment, 2005	25.6	22.5	27.5	24.2
Share of agriculture and forestry in total employment, 2005	5.4	10.5	18.2	8.0
Share of services in total employment, 2005	62.5	59.0	47.8	59.0
% share of private sector in GDP, 2005	86.0	–	87.0	80.0
Inflation rate, 2005	6.0	7.5	6.8	8.0
Net foreign debt as % of GDP	6.6	21.1	10.3	16.8
Net foreign debt as % of exports	32.2	57.7	77.0	60.0
debt service as % of exports, 2005	3.0	5.2	6.9	5.1
Budget deficit as % of GDP, 2005	2.5	3.0	6.0	0.0
Unemployment rate, 2005	5.0	11.7	11.6	8.0

Source: Gorzelak *et al.* (1994)

Table 1.3 presents the most optimistic development which might happen in the four Visegrad countries until the year 2005 (according to the prospects formulated by the international experts within the 'Eastern and Central Europe 2000' project).

A cumulative effect of the official GDP decline during the period 1989–1993 is as follows: Poland, -15 per cent; Hungary, -21 per cent; Czech Republic, -21 per cent; Slovakia, -28 per cent. Due to rapid growth of the 'grey economy', actual decline has been lower by a few percentage points. In any case, Central Europe presents much better results than other post-socialist countries (for example, the decline of the GDP in the same period amounted to 45% in Russia, 41% in Bulgaria, 40% in Albania and 37% in the Ukraine).

In all Central European countries agriculture has been the sector most exposed to foreign competition, which the Central European agriculture had to lose. In Poland this was due to its ineffectiveness and subsidies paid to producers of food in countries exporting their agricultural products to Poland. Overproduction of food (in relation to domestic demand) had already emerged in 1990 and was aggravated by a good harvest in 1991. As a result, farmers withdrew from increasing production, which is reflected in data for 1992. This drop was also due to an almost total collapse of large state-owned agricultural enterprises. In effect, farmers were the socio-professional group which lost most during the transformation. In other Central European countries, where agriculture used to be entirely collectivised (i.e. remained either in the hands of the state or constituted co-operative ownership), the problems of agricultural organisation relied on both adjustment to smaller demand and changing the structure (in Poland this last factor affected only some 25% of agriculture).

In general, the economic situation of the four Central European countries in 1992 can be presented in a very concise form in Figure 1.3. The Czech economy is the most balanced, but the least dynamic. Poland presents the opposite characteristics. Foreign debt and inflation (both considerably below the region's average) are the biggest problems of the Czech Republic. Slovakia's situation is worse, mainly due to the high unemployment rate and the budget deficit (the latter still below the region's average). Hungary suffers more tension than the Czech and Slovak republics, mainly because it has the highest budget deficit of the four, a high unemployment rate (also above the average), a foreign debt burden and inflation (both high, but below average for these four countries). Poland's indicators are less than the average for the four countries, especially in terms of foreign debt, and more than average for inflation and budget deficit. Only the unemployment rate in Poland does not differ significantly from the average.

Foreign Investment and Foreign Trade

Economic and legal conditions created for foreign investors have been evaluated as favourable.[1] The facts are that Poland presents the largest potential market, that it has been able to create an institutional framework for foreign and domestic

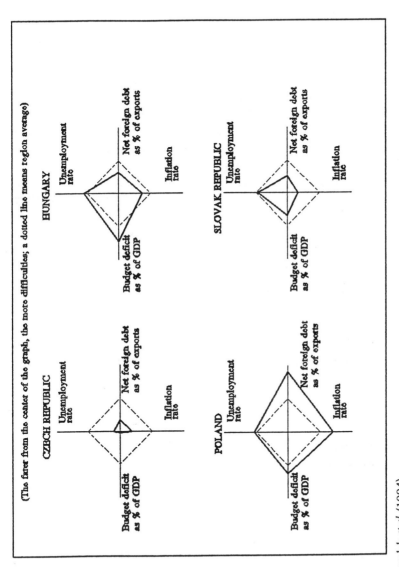

Source: Gorzelak *et al.* (1994)

Figure 1.3 Major imbalances in the Central European economies, 1992

capital and its labour force demonstrates relatively high skills. When these factors are taken into account, it becomes clear why foreign capital views Poland with growing – though still modest – interest.

In a study conducted recently by an independent institute,[2] the Central and Eastern European countries were evaluated from the point of view of investment risk and market attractiveness. In an overall ranking Poland came fourth, after the former GDR, Hungary and the Czech Republic and before Slovakia, Slovenia, Rumania and Bulgaria. It is interesting to note that the highest risk in Poland was attributed to political and social factors (in this second case Poland was considered as the most risky country), and the least risk came from economic factors.

In the period 1990–1992 foreign capital invested or committed in Poland amounted, in consecutive years, to 374 million, 694 million and over 1300 million US dollars, respectively (see Table 1.4 for the origins of foreign capital invested in Poland). It is striking to note that German capital is so poorly represented in Poland, which is against the expectations (or concerns) that Germany would soon invest billions in this country (the same applies to German investment in Slovakia – it amounted only to 76 million US dollars, compared to 76 million US dollars

Table 1.4 Inflow of foreign capital to Poland by country of origin, 1991–1993 (estimate)

Countries	Capital invested (million US dollars)
USA	1050
International	245
Italy	220
The Netherlands	210
Germany	203
Austria	195
France	180
Sweden	80
Great Britain	78
Switzerland	40
Spain	30
Norway	30
Canada	20
Japan	10

Source: Rzeczpospolita, 2 April 1994 (based on data from Central Planning Office and Polish Agency for Foreign Investment).

---

1   On regulations referring to foreign capital and its activities in Poland see Mync 1993.
2   'The map of investment risk', project financed by Polski Bank Rozwoju, conducted by Instytut Badan nad Gospodarka Rynkowa, Warsaw-Gdansk, February 1994.

which arrived from Austria; also in the Czech Republic). By the end of 1993 the total inflow of foreign investment amounted to some 3 billion dollars, and by mid-1995 to 5.4 billion dollars.

This acceleration was the result of several factors: the stabilisation of the general political and economic situation, the changing attitudes of foreign investors towards Central European countries and, last but not least, the introduction of more favourable rules and conditions for foreign investors. According to the present law there are very few restrictions for establishing a company with foreign capital in Poland (no restrictions on the amount of capital to be invested), all profits may be repatriated and tax reliefs are possible in several cases. Comparison of Poland, the Czech and Slovak republics, and Hungary indicates that these four countries all offer similar conditions for foreign investors,[3] though Hungary from the very beginning enjoys favour with the investors.

Table 1.5 presents major foreign investors who have established their activities in 1992 on Polish territory. Foreign investment made in Poland in 1992 presented in this table equalled more than 1.3 billion US dollars already committed and further 2.5 billion US dollars planned in the future in connection with activities already undertaken in this country. It has to be stressed that this table presents the biggest investors only – and several smaller ones have brought considerable capital in, as well.

In other Central European countries the presence of major foreign investors with international capital is also clearly visible. Until the end of 1993 the overall inflow of foreign capital to Hungary has been estimated 6 billion US dollars, 3 billion to the Czech Republic and 0.5 billion to the Slovak Republic. In 1992 only about 15 per cent of foreign capital invested in former Czecho-Slovakia was located in the Slovak part and these proportions have not changed after the split of the federation.

In Hungary foreign investment is being made by bigger investors. By the end of 1993 the greatest ventures with foreign capital in Hungary were the following: General Electric, 550 million US dollars; Volkswagen-Audi, 420 million; US West International, 330 million; General Motors, 300 million; Suzuki, 250 million.

The structure of foreign trade has changed dramatically over the last three years. The Polish situation in this respect is very typical of other Central European countries. Table 1.6 presents basic sectoral and geographical structures of Polish exports in 1989–1991 and Table 1.7 a more general picture for all four countries.

---

3 See Dziemianowicz (1993) for a comparative analysis of regulations and conditions created for foreign capital, magnitude of investment, structure of capital by sectors and by countries of origin and also its regional distribution in all three countries.

Table 1.5 Major foreign investment made in Poland in 1992

Investor	Type of activity	Investment made (mln US $)	Investment planned (mln US $)
FIAT (Italy)	passenger cars	260	1760
Coca Cola (USA)	beverages	180	50
Polish–American Entrepreneurship Fund (USA)	capital co-operation with the private sphere	164	63
Thomson (France)	TV sets and components	147	37
IPC (USA)	paper products	140	175
EDRD (international)	banking system and co-operation with firms	130	0
IFC (international)	industrial investment	123	0
Mariott (USA)	hotels	120	0
ABB (international)	machinery, energy	100	20
Warimpex (Austria)	hotels	100	80
Curtis International (USA)	electronics and construction	100	0
Unilever (international)	home chemistry, food	96	0
Epstein Engineering (USA)	construction, food co-operation with firms	90	110
Procter & Gamble (USA)	home chemistry	60	130
Philips (The Netherlands)	electrotechnics	60	26.5
ING Bank (The Netherlands)	banking	56	0
PpsiCo (USA)	food	55	55
Financing Cimenteries (Italy)	construction, cement industry	55	0
CBR (international)	construction	54	33
Nestle (Switzerland)	food	50	0

Source: Rzeczpospolita, 2 April 1994 (based on data from Central Planning Office and Polish Agency for Foreign Investment)

Table 1.6 Geographical structure of Polish exports, current prices, in percentages

Products	EC 12		European COMECON		Other countries	
	1989	1991	1989	1991	1989	1991
Industry						
• electro-mechanical	14.8	44.3	56.0	28.3	29.2	27.5
• fuel and energy	36.4	39.6	25.3	17.5	38.4	43.0
• metallurgic	55.6	67.2	12.0	5.4	32.5	27.4
• chemical	29.5	39.5	33.4	26.2	36.9	34.2
• mineral	36.9	73.3	11.5	10.6	51.5	16.3
• timber and paper	60.4	76.2	6.1	1.4	33.5	22.5
• light	39.2	63.7	18.7	11.5	42.1	24.9
• food-processing	57.8	64.0	5.0	10.0	37.2	25.9
Construction	13.0	57.8	53.5	25.0	33.5	17.5
Agricultural products	68.0	66.9	17.1	19.2	14.9	14.0
Total exports	32.1	55.6	34.8	16.8	33.1	27.6

Source: Marczewski 1992, p.118.

Table 1.7 Exports structure by main foreign markets

	Czech Rep.	Hungary	Poland	Slovak Rep.
Exports structure 1989 (in %)[a]				
European Community	26	35	38	26
Central Europe	21	15	14	21
Eastern Europe	30	22	18	30
Other	24	28	30	24
Exports structure 1992 (in %)				
European Community	42	50	48	22
Central Europe	25	6	7	54
Eastern Europe	16	14	15	12
Other	17	30	30	12

Note: [a] in 1989 Czechoslovak structure for both Czech and Slovak republics.
Source: G. Gorzelak et al. (1994), Table 1.6.

The message from both these tables is clear. The Central European economies have shifted their exports from the former European COMECON and, to some degree, from other (mainly Third World) countries, to the countries of the European Union. In general, it was not entirely the choice of these countries themselves, however. The former 'Eastern' markets closed down, for various reasons, almost totally in 1990. In the case of the former Soviet Union it was the collapse of its economic system. In the case of more advanced post-socialist economies it was the result of their opening to the West and their decision to import products technologically more advanced (in 1992 Czecho-Slovakia participated in 4–5% and Hungary in less that 1% of Polish foreign trade). As is widely known, losing the Eastern markets created severe economic difficulties, especially for branches oriented towards these particular parts of the world.

There has also been another important change in the structures of Polish foreign trade, i.e. rapid growth of the private sector. While in 1990 its share exports amounted to 4.9 per cent, in 1991 it reached 21.9 per cent of total Polish exports. In imports these figures have changed even more and were equal to 14.4 per cent and 49.9 per cent, respectively.

Foreign debt – amounting to some 48 billion US dollars – is still a heavy burden for the Polish economy. Even in spite of debt reductions (agreements with the Paris Club in 1991 and the London Club in March 1993) its relation to total exports amounted to 3.8, i.e. it was much higher than the commonly accepted 'safety limit'. The Czech Republic is in the most comfortable situation in this respect (compare Figure 1.4).

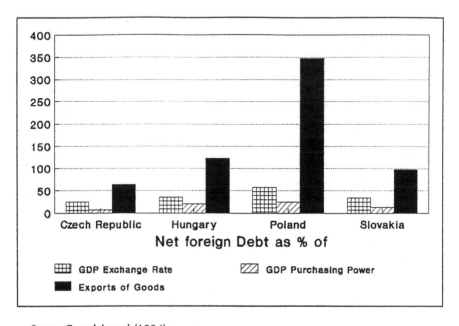

Source: Gorzelak *et al.* (1994)

Figure 1.4 Debt burden of the Central European countries

Structural Changes

Economic restructuring – although not as fast as assumed – has proceeded throughout the entire period. Two 'sides' of this process should, however, be distinguished:

- the collapse of several enterprises in all economic sectors, which has not always reflected their real economic situation and growth potential, but often has been the result of external conditions (mainly the collapse of traditional markets and the 'debt trap');
- the growth of old firms and establishing new economic units, mostly in progressive economic sectors.

Table 1.8 presents the changes in main sectoral structures of the GDP creation in Poland during 1989–1992. As can be seen from the table, we observe a constant decline of agriculture in the creation of the GDP, a growth of the share of industry and very high growth of the share of 'other sectors', i.e. services. It is difficult to judge if the growth of the share of industry will be maintained in the future, although it would be unlikely. Perhaps this tendency for the period 1989–1991 was a temporary result of 'filling the empty space' opened by the decline in agriculture.

Table 1.8 Creation of GDP in Poland, by sectors, 1989–1992

Sectors	Share in creation of GDP[a]					
	1989	1990	1991	1992	1993[b]	1994[b,c]
Industry	41.0	43.6 36.2	39.2	39.6	33.4	33.0
Construction	9.6	9.5 9.3	10.9	11.2	6.6	5.0
Agriculture and forestry	12.2	7.3 13.8	8.4	7.3	6.6	6.0
Other	37.2	39.6 40.7	41.5	41.9	53.4	56.0

Note: [a] 1989 and upper figure for 1990: constant prices 1985; lower figure for 1990–1992: constant prices 1990.
[b] European Classification of Activities: current prices.
[c] estimate

Source: Rocznik Statystyczny (Statistical Yearbook) 1992, 1993.

These changes reflect rationalisation of the overall structure of the Polish economy which has already taken place during the first three years of transformation, though they also indicate the distance between the Polish economy and the more advanced economies of the West – with the important exception of the role of agriculture, which in Poland (as the only socialist country) has not been collectivised since 1948. The Polish case is typical for other post-socialist countries. Table 1.9 presents comparisons of the main economic structures for the four countries.

Table 1.9 Structure of value added and of employment by branches in 1992

	Czech Republic	Hungary	Poland	Slovakia
Total GDP	100.0	100.0	100.0	100.0
• Mining and quarrying	2.8	2.7	2.4	1.6
• Agriculture and forestry	5.1	8.5	6.8	6.6
• Manufacturing	50.4	28.9	46.6	46.4
• Construction	8.4	6.0	7.1	9.5
• Services	33.3	53.9	37.1	36.0
Total employment	100.0	100.0	100.0	100.0
• Mining and quarrying	2.8	1.3	3.1	0.9
• Agriculture and forestry	8.3	13.5	33.8	12.0
• Manufacturing	37.9	27.2	22.3	32.4
• Construction	5.3	6.0	6.2	10.0
• Services	45.7	51.8	34.6	44.7

Source: Gorzelak *et al.* (1994), Table 1.4

The sectoral structure of employment in Poland has also changed. This is illustrated in Table 1.10.

**Table 1.10 Sectoral structure of working
in Poland, 1990–1992 (yearly averages)**

Years	Total number of working (1000s)	Economic sector					
		Industry		Construction		Agriculture	
		1000s	%	1000s	%	1000s	%
1990	16,511	4620	28.0	1243	7.5	4425	26.8
1991	15,601	4250	27.2	1116	7.2	4265	27.3
1992	14,974	3822	25.9	1066	7.1	4037	27.0

Note: Data represent yearly averages (not fully comparable with the state for 31 December)

Comparing Poland with other Central European countries clearly leads to a conclusion of delayed modernisation processes in the biggest country of the region. It is envisaged that in 2005 the employment structures in these countries will be as indicated in Table 1.11.

Table 1.11 Employment by main economic sectors, 1992–2005

| | Czech Republic | | Hungary | | Poland | | Slovakia | |
	1992	2005	1992	2005	1992	2005	1992	2005
Total employment	100.0	100.0	100.0	100.0	100.0	100.0	100.0	100.0
• Mining and quarrying	2.8	1.2	1.4	1.0	3.1	1.1	0.9	0.4
• Agriculture and forestry	8.3	5.4	19.6	10.5	33.8	18.2	12.0	8.0
• Manufacturing	37.9	25.6	25.2	22.5	22.3	27.5	32.4	24.2
• Construction	5.3	5.3	6.9	7.0	6.2	5.4	10.0	8.4
• Services	45.7	62.5	46.9	59.0	34.6	47.8	44.7	59.0

Source: Gorzelak et al. (1994)

The traditional high share of agriculture in the overall structure of employment will remain the most characteristic feature of Poland over the next 10–15 years. This fact will not allow for a rapid shift towards the tertiary sector. Poland will still be a country in which agriculture will be the main reservoir of labour which would flow to non-agricultural occupations. In other post-socialist countries, which had collectivised agriculture by the mid-1950s, the structural shift will take place between industry and services, similar to the processes which took place fairly recently in other developed countries.

Industrial Restructuring

Important structural changes occurred in Polish industry during 1990–1993. Particular industrial branches have performed in divergent ways. In general, most of them have suffered deep decline in 1990 and 1991. In 1992 this situation changed dramatically. Traditional branches of heavy industry have still been in deep decline, while consumer-oriented branches showed substantial growth in 1992. These tendencies continued in the following years. Tables 1.12 and 1.13 present the structural changes in industry which took place during 1990–1992 (Table 1.13 presents the most recent data on the rates of growth which have been recorded in the sales of particular groups of industrial activities. The data is calculated according to the European Classification of Activities, which since 1993 has replaced the former Classification of the National Economy).

Along with the beginning of recovery (which took place somewhere in mid-1992) several branches noted change from negative to positive indices of production dynamics. Data revealed in Table 1.13 demonstrate the roots of Polish recovery. The more technologically advanced the type of manufacturing activity and the more market-oriented, the higher the rates of growth of production during 1993 and the first months of 1994. Traditional branches (mining and quarrying, energy production, basic metal production) demonstrate prolonged negative dynamics, while the sales in the progressive ones grow by 10 per cent.

An especially high rate of growth is demonstrated by sales of construction services. As compared to mere 103–4 per cent of growth during 1991–1992, the growth rates exceeding 150 per cent can be considered as another indication that the recovery has become a stable feature of the Polish economy.

Table 1.12 Growth of sales in Polish industry, by branches
(constant prices, the same period of previous year = 100)

Industrial branches	I–XII 1990	Dynamics of sales I–XII 1991	I–X 1992
Industry, total	75.8	88.1	100.6
• coal	68.2	100.9	90.9
• fuels	79.9	85.4	100.9
• energy	90.3	94.8	95.9
• steel and iron	82.9	76.1	90.0
• non-ferrous metals	76.7	78.9	94.2
• metallic	74.4	87.9	104.7
• machinery	80.4	79.9	84.0
• precise	83.9	74.6	85.0
• means of transport	74.8	66.2	103.6
• electrotechnics and electronic	79.8	83.3	95.4
• chemical	75.4	86.5	100.8
• building materials	80.0	97.6	108.2
• ceramics	78.4	89.7	99.1
• glass	72.2	98.8	100.8
• timber	74.8	99.8	133.0
• paper	76.2	98.0	108.3
• textile	60.4	82.5	92.1
• cloths	76.0	96.9	107.4
• leather	69.4	86.1	91.1'
• food processing	76.3	100.8	107.3
• other	66.4	88.4	103.1
Construction	82.1	104.8	103.1

Source: Chmiel 1992

Table 1.13 Growth of sales in Polish industry, by groups of activities (constant prices, the same period of previous year = 100)

Groups of industrial activities	Dynamics of sales	
	I–XII 1993	I 1994
Industry, total	105.6	109.6
• mining of coal, lignite; extraction of peat	88.4	90.9
• electricity, gas and water supply	81.2	105.2
• food processing, beverages	119.4	108.8
• textiles	107.6	125.6
• basic metals	94.1	115.5
• machinery and equipment	105.3	106.4
• office machinery and computers	167.5	141.4
• motor vehicles, trailers and semi-trailers	121.9	133.3
• electrical machinery and apparatus	110.7	117.6
• radio, TV & communication equipment and apparatus	125.2	104.4
Construction	156.2	144.1

Source: Biuletyn Statystyczny (Statistical Bulletin), GUS, February 1994

The employment structures in Polish industry have also gone through a deep evolutionary process (see Table 1.14). Data on industrial employment for 1993 and the beginning of 1994, compiled according to the principles of European Classification of Activities, support observation concerning the new structure of industrial production dynamics. The highest dynamics of employment in 1993 occurred in market-oriented types of manufacturing such as: wood (122.7%), clothing (122.2%), rubber and plastic products (115.9%), food products and beverages (112.0%), furniture (109.2%), publishing and printing (105.5%); traditional activities like mining and quarrying (reaching in 1993 only 84.2 of the 1992 employment levels) and basic metals (86.6%) noted the greatest losses. These changes provide still more proof of the Polish recovery.

Other activities have also noted a great decrease in employment in 1993. It is surprising to note that the greatest fall of employment occurred in some types of activities which were the most dynamic in terms of production. For example, manufacturing of office equipment and computers employed, in 1993, only 79.5 per cent of the 1992 employment level (and the dynamics of sold production in the same period reached 167.5%, which means more than doubling labour productivity). Manufacturing of motor vehicles and other more complex types of industrial activity, demonstrated in 1993 similar trends, which may lead to the conclusion of accelerated processes of rationalising the most important sectors of the Polish economy.

Table 1.14 Employment in Polish industry, by branches, 1989–1993

Selected branches of industry	Total employment, 1000s				
	1989[a]	1990[a]	1991[b]	1992[b]	1993[b]
industry, total	4052.8	3680.5	3797.8	3452.0	3288.8
• coal mining	489.9	431.4	387.3	370.9	352.2
• production of energy	117.6	119.6	120.9	121.2	123.9
• steel production	144.0	136.0	126.1	119.3	109.4
• machine production	420.6	377.1	345.7	290.8	263.7
• electric and electronic	243.9	225.0	205.8	165.1	147.4
• precision	71.8	65.6	68.1	51.0	44.2
• means of transportation	322.2	296.1	286.5	260.1	248.9
• timber	165.2	141.2	198.3	131.3	185.4
• textile	321.8	285.9	235.9	192.5	175.3
• cloth production	179.8	153.8	222.9	201.7	207.2
• food-processing	410.6	400.4	472.6	480.6	474.2

Note: [a] in establishments owned by the state, co-operatives, trade unions and other public organisations (i.e. excluding private sector)
[b] in all establishments of over 5 employees
[c] in establishments of over 20 employees
Source: Roczni Statystyczny (Statistical Yearbook), 1990–1994

Privatisation

Privatisation has become in Poland, as in other Central European countries, an ideological matter, and not just a problem which should be considered with a business-like approach. Doctrinal assumptions on the faults and merits of the private sphere and its advantages or disadvantages over the public one are considered by some political bodies as a sufficient premise for enforcing or delaying privatisation in Poland, depending on the political profile of the current ruling team.

The privatisation process has undergone its ups and downs. The peak of changes in the ownership structure came in the second half of 1991. At the beginning of the Polish transformation it was conceived as one of the most important factors of economic restructuring. However, scarcity of domestic capital slowed down the process. Several accusations of fraud and mismanagement have also been raised in connection with privatising state enterprises. Political factors played their role, too – for example the J. Olszewski's government (in the first half of 1992) brought privatisation almost to a halt. Privatisation is still looked upon in emotive terms and does not proceed at a pace set by economic reasons. This is particularly true for the so-called 'mass privatisation'. The government proposal of a bill presented to parliament was put down in March 1993 and was only approved as a result of new inter-party agreements and the introduction of some changes. However, its full implementation was then delayed by some months due to new elections called for 19 September 1993. The new coalition of the peasant and social democratic parties has proceeded with privatisation at a remarkable pace, but in turn encountered opposition from the side of the trade unions, and especially the populist-oriented 'Solidarity' trade union, which – being an irony of history – was the main force in dismantling the socialist system in Poland.

Until now, two major forms of privatisation have been used: by liquidation and the so-called 'capital privatisation'. Privatisation by liquidation is being performed in two ways:

- On the basis of article 19 of the law on state enterprises, issued in 1981. In this procedure the existence of a state-owned enterprise as a legal entity may be terminated if it is in difficult economic conditions (these conditions are explicitly specified). In this case the property of such an enterprise may be sold or leased (for 5 to 10 years), usually in parts; very often these assets are bought or rented by small companies established by former employees of this enterprise. We shall refer to this way of privatisation as to a L1-type.

- On the basis of article 37 of the law on privatisation of state enterprises, issued on 13 July 1990. In this case a state-owned enterprise is liquidated by selling off its assets in an 'organised' form to an external buyer; very often the company, established by the employees of this particular enterprise, buys or leases the assets. This road of privatisation by liquation is being applied to enterprises in sound economic condition. This we shall call the L2-type privatisation.

The 'capital privatisation', based on articles 5 and 6 of the law on privatisation of state-owned enterprises is based on the following procedure: a state enterprise (which has to be in good economic condition) becomes a company of the State Treasury and then it issues shares. In the case of 186 enterprises that were registered as of special importance for the state, the privatisation procedure should have the approval of the Council of Ministers. If over 50 per cent of shares are sold to private owner(s), the enterprise is considered to be privatised. In some cases they are offered on the stock exchange.[4] Usually, the employees have the right to buy some part of these shares at a reduced price.

4　The Polish stock exchange passed a full cycle: from neglect and suspicion at its very beginning in 1991, to enthusiasm and national sport at the end of 1993, back again to frustration and disbelief after the shock of spring 1994. At its best the turnover of one session reached 10 billion ziotys (approx 500 million US dollars) and the index exceeded 20,000. After the crisis which started on 17 March 1994 the index fell twofold, to a level of 7000 – some say due to a self-fulfilling prophecy by Stanley Morgan consultancy – and has not exceeded the value of 9000 since then. In any case, the Warsaw stock exchange has rooted itself in social consciousness, thus becoming the most popular, nation-wide educational facility in modern economics and business. It has also became an important source of capital for Polish companies which have issued their shares.

During the period from 1 August 1990 to 31 December 1993, 2521 state enterprises have been privatised in Poland, which constitutes 30 per cent of the total number of state enterprises existing in 1990. A further 1595 state farms were liquidated and handed over to the State Agricultural Property Agency and 263 enterprises were municipalised. All in all, a change in ownership took place in more than half of the original number of 8,441 enterprises which belonged to the state at the end of 1990.

In 1999 enterprises a liquidation process has either been completed or is underway (1082 of L1-type, 917 of L2-type). By the end of 1993, 522 state companies became companies of the State Treasury (in consecutive years these numbers were as follows: 1991, 221 firms; 1992, 220; 1993, only 47). By the end of 1993, 98 firms were fully privatised by the 'capital' route and a further 100 awaited movement into the private sector via this procedure.

As already mentioned, no general, voucher-type privatisation has been introduced in Poland; however, according to the most recent legislation, the so-called 'Common Programme of Privatisation' will soon be implemented. It assumes that the State Treasury would become the owner of some 200 state enterprises (usually in good economic conditions). These enterprises would be managed by 20–25 investment funds. Coupons issued by these funds, covering the value of these enterprises, would be available free of charge (only a registration fee would be collected) to all adults in the country. The owners of the coupons would be allowed to sell them freely. It is envisaged that after some time the market would decide on the real value of coupons issued by particular investments funds which, in turn, would allow for estimating the market value of enterprises belonging to these funds.

In April 1994, 23 privatised firms offered their shares on the Warsaw stock market (banks, breweries, construction-design firms, foreign trade companies, producers of electric appliances and materials, cloth/shoe-producing companies, the most famous producer of confectionary, a producer of paint and a producer of furniture). Several other companies are waiting to enter the stock exchange and in mid-1995 this number had more than doubled. Foreign capital – already present here – looks at the Polish stock exchange with growing interest, though is still worried by its instability and immaturity.

Table 1.15 presents the structure of Polish privatisation, by sectors. Differences between particular sectors are clear. Agriculture appeared to be the weakest sector and had to go through the L1-type privatisation by liquidation. In fact, the state farms have not been bought all that frequently, which is due to several factors: the low profitability of farming, the poor economic condition of these farms and a lack of local capital. Communications are in an entirely different situation, due to high profitability induced by the vast unsatisfied demand for services in this sector. Construction firms used to be bought or leased by small employees' companies, which was also the case with establishments operating in trade.

Table 1.15 Privatisation in Poland by type
and sector, 1.08.1990–31.03.1992

| Sectors | Total | Type of privatisation | | |
		Capital	Liquidation L1-type	L2-type
Total	100.0	27.2	40.9	31.4
• Industry	100.0	53.7	30.5	15.8
• Construction	100.0	15.5	27.6	56.9
• Agriculture	100.0	0.5	88.8	10.7
• Forestry	100.0	66.7	33.3	–
• Transport	100.0	12.2	73.2	14.6
• Communication	100.0	–	–	100.0
• Trade	100.0	0.7	38.6	. 60.7
• Other	100.0	4.2	39.4	56.4

Source: Prywatyzacja przedsiebiorstw panstwowych (Privatisation of state enterprises), Central Statistical Office, Warsaw 1992, Table 5

In effect, by the end of 1992 over 50 per cent of the economically active population are working in the private sphere, out of which approximately half work outside agriculture. Several branches, like services and trade, have been privatised almost entirely.

Table 1.16 presents the changes in the ownership structure of the Polish economy which took place during the years 1989–1992.

Table 1.16 Working in the public sphere as a percentage
of total number working in the Polish economy

| Sector | Shares (in %) | | | | Differences (% points) |
	1989	1990	1991	1992	1992–1989
Total	52.8	50.0	44.5	42.3	-10.5
• Industry	70.9	68.8	64.2	59.5	-11.4
• Construction	62.6	57.9	40.5	28.1	-34.5
• Agriculture	11.9	10.5	8.0	6.0	-5.9
• Trade	27.9	17.8	11.7	9.3	-18.0

Source: Rocznik Statystyczny (Statistical Yearbook), 1990–1993

As can be seen, 1991 brought the acceleration of privatisation. The fastest decline of the share of the public sphere took place in construction and in domestic trade. This last sector became, in 1991, almost entirely privatised, while the share of the public sphere in industry was almost 50 per cent.

Table 1.17 Dynamics of the number of working in Poland, by sectors and ownership, 1989–1991

Sectors	Total	Public	Private	Total	Public	Private	Total	Public	Private
	1990, 1989 = 100			1991, 1990 = 100			1991, 1989 = 100		
Total	93.8	86.6	102.3	96.3	85.5	107.0	90.3	74.1	109.5
• Industry	88.6	85.9	95.2	91.3	84.8	106.1	80.9	72.9	100.9
• Construction	88.8	81.9	100.3	96.8	67.6	137.0	85.9	55.4	137.4
• Agriculture	96.8	85.3	98.4	96.6	70.8	99.8	93.5	60.4	98.2
• Domestic trade	100.7	65.7	113.9	116.0	75.5	124.9	116.8	46.9	142.3

Source: Rocznik Statystyczny (Statistical Yearbook), 1990–1993.

Table 1.17 clearly indicates that the changes in the ownership structures were mainly due to the decline of the public sphere and – in some sectors – to the growth of the private sector. Domestic trade and construction had the fastest growth of employment in the private sphere, while in industry this employment was stable and in agriculture it even declined (though in a slower pace than in the public sphere).

The private sector has the largest share in Poland of all Central European economies (see Figure 1.5). This is due to two main factors: traditionally, Poland had the greater share of agriculture, which used to be predominantly private, and the fast process of privatisation after 1989.

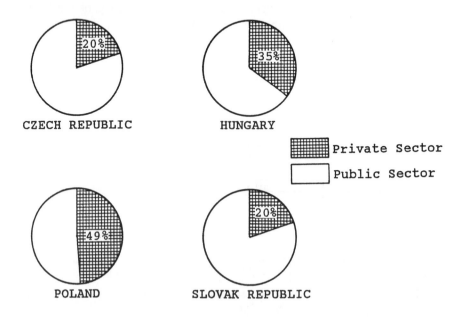

Figure 1.5 The share of the private sector in GDP, 1992

There are no reliable estimates of the 'black sector' of the Polish economy. Figures in the range of 20–30 per cent of the GDP are quoted, however, without any sound basis of proof. To some extent too restrictive a fiscal policy of the state pushes some economic activity 'underground' leading to a kind of vicious circle (less revenue for the state budget – higher taxes – growth of hidden economic activity – higher taxes etc.). The following relation exemplifies the result of this 'game': the private sphere, which employs over 50 per cent of the total workforce, provides only 4 per cent of all tax revenue. This is due to the fact that private firms 'pump' costs (by purchasing or leasing expensive cars, luxurious office equipment etc.) in order to avoid taxes. It can be partly explained by the mistakes made by central government – for example no tax relief on profits spent on new investment has been introduced. Estimates made demonstrate that such relief, through activating underutilised production, would result in an increase of tax revenue. It can be hoped that new measures will be introduced which will strengthen the private sector and in this way the entire Polish economy.

The Labour Market

Obviously, there are also several negative sides of the transformation processes. Pauperisation and unemployment have hit wide strata of the population, resulting in worsening of both the level and the structure of consumption. Unemployment is the most common and painful manifestation of these costs.

In December 1991 the population of Poland was 38,309,000, out of which almost 30 per cent were in the pre-working age bracket (under 18) and almost 13 per cent in the post-work age bracket (men: 65+, women: 60+). There were 22,055,000 of a working age. The 'dependency ratio' amounted to 74 per cent. The economic activity rates have been dropping since the late 1970s (for data of 1988 and 1992 see Table 1.18). Data for 1992 represent the situation in May, as measured by a sample survey of households. In all categories but one we notice constant falls in activity rates. Women in towns are the only exception. Its

Table 1.18 Economic activity rates in Poland, 1988, 1992

Categories	Years	Total	Men	Women
Total	1988	65.1	74.3	57.0
	1992	61.4	69.9	53.7
Towns	1988	61.2	70.3	53.1
	1922	59.0	67.7	57.3
Rural	1988	71.8	80.3	63.5
areas	1992	65.6	74.2	51.6

Source: Aktywnosc zawodowa i bezrobocie w Polsce (Economic Activity and unemployment in Poland), GUS, Warsaw 1992, Table 3.2

explanation seems to be simple: in the new, difficult economic situation women start to seek jobs in order to bolster the family budget. This holds true for women in the 35–54 age bracket, i.e. after their maternal responsibilities are over.

The decrease in the number of jobs due to the economic recession manifested itself from the very beginning of the transformation period (see Table 1.19).

Table 1.19 Number of working people in Poland, 1989–1993 (31 December)

Years	Total in 1000s	Type of ownership			
		Public		Private	
		1000s	%	1000s	%
1989	17,558.8	9546.1	55.7	7583.7	44.3
1990	16,511.4	8941.9	54.20	7569.5	45.8
1991	15,326.4	7633.0	49.8	7693.4	50.2
1992	14,676.6	6799.9	46.3	7876.7	53.7
1993	14,330.1	6183.5	43.2	8146.6	56.8

Source: Rocznik Statystyczny (Statistical Yearbook) 1993, Table 1; 1994, Table 1

Two tendencies are evident: a decrease in the number of those working in the national economy and a shift from the public to the private sector. The total number of jobs lost during the three years 1990–1993 amounted to over 2 million. The public sector shed over 2.6 million, but 600,000 new jobs have been gained in the private sector. It should also be noted that within the private sector 200,000 persons moved from agriculture to non-agricultural occupations, which means that the private sector was able to create over 800,000 new jobs outside agriculture.

The difference between the economically active and the work available constitutes *unemployment*. This is one of the most grave effects of the transformation process in Poland. According to the most recent data (beginning of 1994), there have been 2,959,000 registered unemployed in Poland, which is 2.4 points more than in January 1993 (the overall growth of the number of unemployed during the entire 1993 reached 15.2%). The unemployment rate reached 16 per cent of the total number of the civilian economically active population. More than 550,000 of the currently unemployed lost jobs due to the problems of their former employers (group lay-offs, liquidation of an enterprise etc.).

The situation on the non-rural labour market was much more serious. The number of all registered unemployed constituted 25 per cent of all economically active people outside agriculture. There are estimates that in this last sector some 700,000 persons are only partly employed, which adds to the overall dramatic picture of the labour market in Poland. Agriculture became a kind of a reservoir for those who had lost jobs in nearby towns and could not find any other employment. By this process the chances for achieving by 10–15 years in Poland a modern structure of employment, with low shares of agriculture, are decreasing.

Around 30 per cent of the total number of unemployed did not receive unemployment benefits. Women constitute more than half of this group. Almost 650,000 unemployed (21.2% of the total number of unemployed) have never worked before, 202,000 of them were graduates who left school in 1993. University graduates constituted 4.5 per cent of this group, and those who left vocational schools (11 years of schooling), almost one half.

Almost one-third of the unemployed have attained only primary or lower levels of education. A further one-third without work have basic vocational training and only 2.5 per cent have attained a university degree. On average, the probability of becoming unemployed is five times lower for a university graduate than for an employee with only basic skills. The structure of the unemployed, according to their educational level, demonstrates the role which the level of education has begun to play in the Polish economy – this is a clear change of old patterns according to which a higher level of education has not necessarily led to a higher living standard and social status. The number of long-term unemployed grows, which indicates that unemployment in Poland is of a structural character. In June 1992, 33 per cent of the unemployed had lived without work for more than 9 months. In December 1993 the share of unemployed for a period longer than 12 months reached 45 per cent.

According to 'soft' estimates, in Poland some 20–40 per cent of the registered unemployed have never worked or do work unofficially, thus adding to the 'grey' economy. This figure is not greatly different from such estimates in other Central European countries.

In spite of a dramatic increase in unemployment in Poland during 1990–1993, the phenomenon of excessive employment persists, especially in industry. In 1991 it was estimated at approximately 950,000–1.5 million. The overall decrease of industrial production was twice as high as the decrease in industrial employment. State enterprises are still reluctant to adjust the number of employees to the actual level of production, since they expect improvement of their economic situation and do not want to lose often highly qualified specialists. Moreover, the enterprises are still perceived as institutions which should perform social functions and the pressure to maintain a high level of employment is strong.

Poland is not the only Central European country facing the problem of unemployment. By the end of 1992 the unemployment rates were 2.6 in the Czech Republic, 11.5 in Slovakia and 13.7 in Hungary. Figures 1.6 and 1.7 present comparative data for the four countries.

Social Costs

The economic reform resulted in greater social polarisation. The unemployed are obviously in the worst situation. But also those who have work very often cannot maintain their standard of living. These processes are explained by the growth of differentiation in incomes (see Table 1.20). In fact, differentiation of incomes is

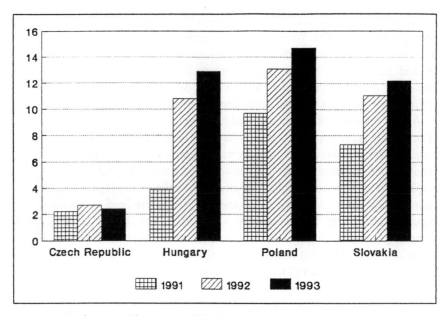

Source: Employment Observatory, CEC, No 5

Figure 1.6 Unemployment rates in Central Europe

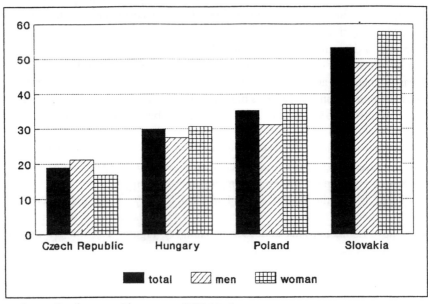

Source: Employment Observatory, CEC, No 5

Figure 1.7 Percentage of long-term unemployed in total unemployment

much deeper, since the family budget surveys do not capture the lowest and the highest incomes. They also do not measure incomes generated in the black economy, which definitely concentrate in the highest fractions of income distribution. By all estimates this process has persisted in 1992 and 1993, and will continue in the future. However, relative improvement of incomes earned by the highly educated should be considered as a positive effect of the transformation.

Table 1.20 Differentiation of personal incomes of employees in Poland, 1989–1991

Years	Income share of The lowest 5%	The highest 5%
1989	2.48	5.80
1990	4.78	6.05
1991	4.24	6.24

Source: Kudrycka 1992, p.143

Living conditions have deteriorated mainly as a result of a decrease in real incomes. Moreover, state subsidies for several social services, such as recreation, child care (nurseries, kindergartens etc.) have been withdrawn almost entirely. This caused a shift from a situation of permanent shortage of social infrastructure and social services to a situation in which supply of these services is greater than the real demand.

The same situation applies to housing. In spite of the large unsatisfied demand for dwellings (there are some 120 households for 100 dwellings), high interest in newly built apartments (previously in a great part covered by the state), pushes the prices of new housing up to an unaffordable level for an average-income family. New co-operative flats stay unoccupied. The government has proposed some new measures which aim to solve this problem, but in any case they are insufficient in a situation of budgetary crisis and tremendous social needs.

The Transformation of Central Europe: A Prospective View

The economic scenarios for all Central European countries – as presented in the most synthetic form in Table 1.3 – are strongly *growth oriented*. Investment efforts and replacement of old and obsolete fixed assets of low technical standard by new equipment, are the basic assumptions behind the scenarios. The possibility of high growth rates in the long run without an appropriate level of investment were rejected. A high efficiency rate of return for the investment process seems to be indispensable if the programme is to be feasible.

The scenarios assume slower growth of consumption than of GDP. Fixed capital formation will note the highest rates of growth. Public consumption is assumed to grow at a slower pace.

The Czech Republic will demonstrate the slowest, but the most balanced path of growth. The budget deficit will be the lowest there (2.5% of GDP), as well as the inflation rate (6.0) and the burden of foreign debt. Hungary, and especially Poland, will demonstrate more rapid, but also more unbalanced, patterns of growth.

Fast growth will necessarily lead to *structural change*, since it will not occur in all sectors of the Central European economies at the same pace. In effect, the sectoral structures would resemble in 2005 present economic structures of the western rural lands of Germany. The primary sectors will be the greatest losers and the share of agriculture and forestry in the overall employment structure will fall below 5.5 per cent in the Czech Republic, though in Poland this sector will still keep a much larger share of total employment (18.4%). With the exception of Poland – where this share will be lower by some 10 points – services are likely to accommodate 60 per cent of total employment.

The overall growth of the working population will amount to over 2 million during 1992–2005, reaching 26.6 million in 2005. *Unemployment* will still be one of the most difficult problems of the three Central European economies (i.e. with the exception of the Czech Republic) and it appears that this problem will not be solved in the time envisaged in the scenario, even if a high rate of growth is achieved. In Poland alone the number of unemployed will reach 2.4 million and overall unemployment in the four countries will approach 3.5 million. In Poland and Hungary the unemployment rate will exceed 11.5 per cent and only in the Czech Republic is it likely to remain at the more civilised level of 5 per cent.

A reduced access to the EU market may cause an important slowdown in economic growth. Favourable economic relations with other countries appear to be of crucial importance for the assumed path of development.

Post-Fordism or Post-Communism? The Nature of Post-Socialist Transformation

It has been generally assumed that the changes occurring in the post-socialist countries result almost entirely from the shift from the centrally planned economic system supported by a mono-party regime to a market economy introduced in a democratic political system. This approach stresses the 'ideological' or systemic factors of the post-socialist transformation.

If this approach is correct, then the post-socialist transformation should be regarded as a unique phenomenon, specific only to the transition from a communist (or so called 'real socialism') system to market economy. Since no other experience of this type can be met in the history of humankind, no processes similar to these currently observed in post-socialist part of Europe should be met elsewhere.

However, even simple reflection reveals that these assumptions do not hold true. In fact, the restructuring processes that dominate in the post-socialist transformation very strongly resemble the phenomena which shaped the economic life in more advanced Western countries since the 1960s and specially during the 1970s.

This thesis can be substantiated in different fields. In the material sphere the decline of traditional industries which begun to happen in Central Europe after 1990 (with the exception of Hungary, when the first decline in coal mining occurred in the mid-1980s)[5] is nothing else but delayed by 20 to 30 years' repetition of the industrial restructuring which was begun in the West in early 1960s and was accelerated in the 1970s.

In the non-material sphere the reliance on the centre and lack of own initiatives observed in several cases in the regions and localities of Central Europe resembles very much the attitudes prevailing also in the West until the 1970s.

With a great deal of simplification one may say that the post-socialist transformation is a shift from fordist to post-fordist type of organisation of economic, social and political life. This shift was not possible in a closed system, separated by economic and political barriers from the global markets and therefore not exposed to economic and political international competition. Once these barriers were removed, the old patterns of economic production could not longer be maintained and 'imported' patterns of new ways of socio-economic and political organisation begun to shape the new reality. The post-socialist countries 'catch up', at a much faster rate, with the rest of the developed world, more advanced with this restructuring.

If these theses are true, then the post-socialist transformation should be 'de-mythologised' from its ideological underpinnings (although this dimension should not be entirely neglected) and should be regarded as a 'normal' process of technological and organisational change, performed later than it would have happened if Central Europe (and also other socialist countries) had been incorporated earlier into an open global economy. In a similar manner, the decline in economic output which occurred in post-socialist countries after 1990 was a similar price for restructuring to that which the West paid for its change of socio-economic structures after 1973 (as I have argued elsewhere (Gorzelak 1995), the Western recession of the 1970s and early 1980s can be considered as a price the West paid for abandoning the fordist type of economic organisation and developing post-fordist patterns).

The above theses should perhaps be given more consideration once more sound statistical evidence is available after few further years of post-socialist transformation. In any case, there are definitely more resemblances between Western and Eastern restructuring than one could judge if only 'ideological' factors were taken under consideration.

---

5   See Fazekas and Gorzelak 1995.

References

Chmiel, J. (1992) 'Produkcja przemyslowa – przebieg prywatyzacji.' (Industrial production – process of privatisation). In L. Zienkowski (1992) *op.cit.*

Dziemianowicz, W. (1993) 'Foreign capital in Poland, Czecho-Slovakia and Hungary.' In G. Gorzelak and A. Kuklinski (eds) *Dilemmas of regional Policies in Eastern and Central Europe.* Warsaw: EUROREG, vol. 8.

Fazekas, K. and Gorzelak, G. (1995) 'Restructuring and Labour Market in Regions Dominated by Heavy Industry in Central Europe.' In *The Regional Dimension of Unemployment in Transition Countries.* Paris: OECD.

Gorzelak, G., Kuklinski, A., Jalowiecki, B. and Zienkowski, L. (1994) 'Eastern and Central Europe 2000 – Final Report.' Studies 2. DGXII of the European Commission, Luxembourg.

Gorzelak, G. (1995) *Transformacja Systemowa a Restrukturyzacja Regionalna* (Systemic Transformation and Regional Restructing). Warsaw: EUROREG-UNESCO Chair.

Kudrycka, I. (1992) 'Rozklady i zróznicowanie dochodów w latach 1989–1991.' (Distribution and differentiation of incomes in 1989–1991). In Zienkowski (ed) (1992) *op.cit.*

Marczewski, K. (1992) 'Wspólpraca gospodarcza z zagranica w okresie transformacji (Economic foreign co-operation during transformation).' In L. Zienkowski (ed) *Gospodarka Polska w Latach 1990–1992. Doswiadczenia i Wnioski (Polish Economy 1990–1992 – Experiences and Conclusions).* Warsaw: ZBSE GUS i PAN.

Mync (1993) 'Foreign capital in Poland.' In G. Gorzelak and A. Kuklinski (eds) *Dilemmas of Regional Policies in Eastern and Central Europe.* Warsaw: EUROREG., vol. 8.

Rzeczpospolita (1994) 'The prospects according to the estimates of the Institute for Market Economy Research.' 22 April.

CHAPTER 2

The Historic Heritage
of Socio-Economic Space

The Origins

Space and the way it is managed are the most stable factors of human development. This is true even in the case of Poland – a country which has frequently changed its boundaries and which underwent major destructions of its human and physical capital. However, present differentiations of the Polish social and economic spaces can be traced back through several centuries.

The cradle of the Polish nation and the Polish state was located (at the turn of the millennium) in the mid-western part of contemporary Poland, in the region called Wielkopolska (with its centre in Poznan). Within one century Malopolska (with its centre in Kraków) became the next centre of political and economic power. For the next few centuries these two regions constituted the heart of the country. It was only later (from the 14th century) that the economic power of the Hanzeatic harbour city, Gdansk, emerged and it took still two centuries more before Warsaw became the capital of the country, which spurred economic development in this region. In the meantime, Lower Silesia (with Wrocìaw as a major city) was lost, first to the Czech state and then, through Austria, it suffered German domination.

This spatial pattern of Poland, to a large extent, was the result of the location of the country on two major transcontinental commercial routes: the so-called amber route from the South to the North and the East–West route which connected Northern Europe with Asia. Over time both these routes have not lost their importance, though their meaning for social, political and economic processes has evolved. Figure 2.1 presents the historical regionalisation of 10th–12th century Poland (in contemporary boundaries), which has persisted until the present day.

In fact, this particular regional structure has persisted in Poland throughout the entire millennium. The period of partitions (1795–1918) was the only time when a different regional breakdown of Polish territories had been introduced.

In this way we have identified the first historic factor which has shaped the spatial structure of Poland, *the traditional regional division*. The *international* factor is the second one.

Source: Piskozub 1987, p.96

Figure 2.1 Provinces of Poland, 10th–12th centuries

Throughout the centuries Poland has changed (or was forced to change) its boundaries. The thousand years of Polish history may be encapsulated in one phrase: constant pressure from the west and constant pressure and expansion to the east. Only once, in 1945, was Polish state territory moved in the opposite direction – from east to west.

The frontier with different German states has been, throughout the centuries, the most stable international frontier for Poland. Though this frontier has undergone several changes, its impact is still visible on the demographic, economic and social maps of Poland. Figure 2.2 presents its stability during the last 200 years.

Poland re-emerged on the map of Europe as an independent country at the end of World War II, after 123 years of absence from this map. World War II resulted in a major shift of Polish boundaries westwards. The boundaries of Czechoslovakia and Hungary which exist today (or, in the Czecho-Slovak case, have existed till recently) were shaped after World War I. These two countries emerged out of the Austro-Hungarian Empire. Hungary lost two-thirds of its pre-war territory. The full and formal split of Czechoslovakia into two independent countries occurred on 1 January 1993, as the result of political games and, to a lesser extent, as a

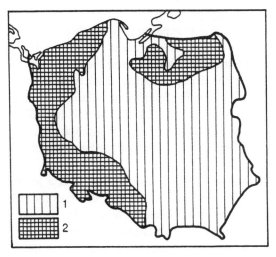

1. Commonwealth of the Two Nations
2. Prussia,1771

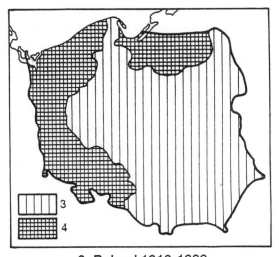

3. Poland,1918-1939
4. Germany,1918-1939

Source: Piskozub 1987, p.147

Figure 2.2 Stability of Polish western border

result of the will of the population. It has had, and will have, important influence on these two newly emerging countries.

All four countries of Central Europe throughout their entire history have been located on the *European economic periphery*. The Czech Republic is most closed to one of the two main European economic axes: the 'old' northern one, extending from London to Rome (the 'European banana'). All of them are far away from the new Mediterranean axis, extending from Milan to Barcelona. Only the Czech lands have experienced an advanced level of capitalist industrialisation. In Poland, Hungary and Slovakia the main wave of industrialisation came along with the socialist system after World War II, which perhaps was most pronounced in Slovakia.

The present spatial structure of Central Europe is a joint product of two processes: long historical trends in building the pattern of the settlement structure and the 19th century industrialisation introduced by the industrial revolution (delayed at the periphery). These two factors have constituted the general spatial organisation of the economies and societies of Central Europe.

The Spatial Economic Patterns

It was only in the 19th century that the foundations of *modern, industrial development* were laid in Poland within the general stream of the industrial-technological revolution. Two major industrial centres emerged: Upper Silesia (at that time being a part of Prussia, then a part of the united German state and in the inter-war period the majority of its territory being in Germany) and Lódz, the centre of the textile industry.

The historic processes created a long-rooted division of the country into two parts: the western, the better developed one, and the eastern, less advanced in economic development. This division has been reinforced by the 123 years of the partition of Poland when it was absent from the map of European states (1795–1918). The shift of the state boundaries to the west in 1945 has not changed this pattern, though the most backward areas became a part of the former Soviet Union.

Poland was lucky to develop a *well-balanced urban network*. There exist some 300 medium-sized towns which successfully play the role of local centres and some 7 to 10 cities which could be called the regional of provincial metropolises. Poland avoided the pattern of a country being dominated by one metropolis or one region, even taking into account the conurbation of Upper Silesia, inhabited by some 4 million people.

The 20th century has not brought major changes into this historically created spatial pattern. The general settlement pattern and the East–West division has been preserved, even in spite of two major attempts to accelerate the development of the backward parts of the Polish territory.

The first such attempt was undertaken in the 1930s, when a major state investment was located in the *Central Industrial District*, which in the pre-war boundaries was located in the heart of the country (within the triangle Rzeszów–Kielce–Lublin). Investment was directed mainly at metallurgy and engineering (a great part constituted by military production), chemical and food-processing industries. World War II terminated the project, though several factories had been completed and function to this day.

The second attempt at levelling out deep regional differences was undertaken within the framework of so-called '*socialist industrialisation*' after 1948. There have been at least two periods (1950–1956, 1966–1970) when the 'equity' principle has taken centre stage in formal state policies. In fact, however, further concentration of economic potential in already developed urban-industrial centres has prevailed, though accelerated development of several peripheral regions should not be neglected. These were mainly the regions which offered the possibility of exploitation of raw materials (coal, sulphur, copper) and this type of economic activity became the major factor in their development.

In pursuit of the type of industrialisation and development which has been predominant in Poland for at least the last two centuries, Poland has produced a clear functional unity of *urbanisation–industrialisation–welfare*. Towns are the sites of industry and industry used to be the main factor responsible for social advancement and infrastructural development. Industry generated personal incomes, which, combined with higher levels of infrastructure, created better living conditions in towns than in rural areas. This pattern is probably typical for countries still dominated by a mechanism of development based on agriculture and industry, with relative underdevelopment of the service sector, or in countries which have undertaken an accelerated effort aimed at changing these dominant economic structures.

Several comparative analyses conducted on Polish territorial units (voivodships, towns, communes) prove that three major factors have been responsible for the structure of Polish socio-economic space:

- the level of industrial and urban development, with the gradient from south west (the highest level) to north east (the lowest). The general direction of the gradient does not exclude, obviously, the existence of several exceptions from the general pattern: Warsaw and Lódz in the centre of the country, or Szczecin in the north western corner, are the most clear examples.

- the historic factor, differentiating Poland in a south east–north west line. This factor distinguishes the regions of different socio-economic composition, in which two structures, demographic and agricultural, are the most important. The north western territories have, generally speaking, a younger population and a much greater share of state or co-operative agriculture, and also a greater share of larger private farms, while in the south eastern part of the country these characteristics are the opposite.

- urban–rural differences, which have already been explained.

Superimposition of all these factors produced a general spatial pattern of Poland: the areas constituting a big 'letter L', beginning in Gdansk, then going south west through Poznan to Wroclaw and turning east through Upper Silesia to Kraków concentrating a vast part of the economic potential of the country. This 'letter L' is, of course, supplemented by some 'islands' like Warsaw, Lódz, Szczecin and much smaller 'peaks' of economic potential in the east (Bialystok, Lublin, Rzeszów).

The 'letter L' pattern was already distinguished in the early 1950s, when spatial analyses of Poland in new, post-war frontiers, have been undertaken. Forty years of the socialist system, under which further concentration of the economic potential proceeded in the already heavily invested regions and industrial centres, have only reinforced this pattern. Poland entered its systemic transformation with this particular spatial structure.

The last observation also holds true for other Central European countries. Socialist industrialisation reshaped the social and economic space of Central Europe to a much lesser extent than the socialist system changed social stratification and social attitudes in this part of Europe. In fact, the general spatial patterns have not been changed in qualitative terms. Paradoxically, one may even say that socialist industrialisation reinforced traditional spatial patterns.

However, several new phenomena emerged in the socio-economic space of Central Europe after World War II. Six main dimensions of spatial change could be distinguished:

- the introduction of 'big' (also of heavy) industry into great cities, which resulted in pronounced changes in their economic and social structures and limiting the development of their service functions;

- the creation of several new industrial centres, which were based on the extraction of raw materials (coal, lignite, copper, sulphur, iron, uranium), and/or on metallurgy and energy production;

- the accelerated industrialisation of traditionally rural areas, in many cases coupled with the growth of mining and heavy industries, which resulted in the growth of middle-sized towns and created a new socio-occupational structure in these areas (a large share of so-called 'bi-professionals' and commuting to work, since the urban system could not fulfil all the requirements of the industrial complex);

- the collectivisation of agriculture, which changed the settlement structure in rural areas and created large state-owned or collective farms, in this way liquidating traditional, family-run farming (Poland was the only exception in this process, though agriculture in western and northern parts of Poland was collectivised, with up to 50 per cent of land in state hands);

- the 'fetish of industrialisation' left limited resources for other economic sectors. This resulted in the relative underdevelopment of infrastructure. Roads and telecommunications were hit most severely. Only railways, essential for transporting the mass products of the mining, heavy industries and agriculture, were developed properly;

- the dramatic deterioration of the quality of the natural environment due to the extremely simplistic attitudes to development and total neglect of other targets of development other than quantitative growth.

As a result, the Central European countries were not able to overcome the traditional pattern of spatial-functional relationships between urbanisation, industrialisation and the level of living, which was possible in more mature economies. Towns were the centres of industry and offered a much higher standard of living. Industry remained the main source of income, social advancement and economic development. *The entire economies of the socialist countries – and especially their regional economies – were clearly industry-driven*, and this industry was totally subordinate to the paradigm of the second technological revolution. Only the Czech lands, owing to their older traditions of industrial civilisation, demonstrated some more mature spatial patterns.

In spite of accelerated industrialisation, the traditional division of all four countries into their *more developed western and less developed eastern parts* has persisted and is still clearly visible. To some extent, only Hungary was the exception to this pattern since it used to be divided into a more developed north and less developed south. However, more recent changes have introduced the general east–west pattern to Hungary also, since the Danube divides the more progressive western part from the slower eastern part. In all four countries several areas are still at a *low level of development*, being poorly equipped with infrastructure, predominantly rural and with a poorly educated labour force.

It was hoped at the beginning of socialist industrialisation that these regional differences would cease to exist. This did not happen, as a result of two factors coming into play:

- industrialisation carried out on the less developed areas was too limited both in magnitude and in the level of diversification of the industrial structure, to produce a basis for self-sustained regional development;

- in fact, a great part (in Poland, the main part) of the industrialisation effort was concentrated in traditional industrial centres, which led to overconcentration of industrial production in many of them and did not allow for alleviating the regional inequalities.

As a result, several territories of the four countries can be labelled as truly '*old industrial areas*'. They present all features of 'industrial backwardness': the mono-functional production structure; a biased structure of skills and educational profiles of the labour force; high levels of pollution; a deteriorating urban substance.

Socialist politics and socialist economies were closed systems. The relative *underdevelopment of the border areas* was the direct spatial outcome of this feature of the socialist reality. The number of border crossings had been small. International transportation routes were underdeveloped. Trans-border co-operation was almost non-existent or – during the last years of the socialist rule – assumed a one-direction pattern (from the West to the East: from Germany to Poland and the Czech Republic, from Austria to Hungary). Traditional ties between regions and cities were almost entirely broken (Vienna–Bratislava, the two cities connected in the past by a tramway and then almost totally separated by the state border, are the most pronounced example of this phenomenon).

The Central European countries entered the challenging phase of transformation with a strongly polarised regional structure and deep spatial inequalities, overindustrialised cities, an underdeveloped infrastructure and a polluted environment. Several new processes emerged during the first four years of this transformation, thus giving the first indications of the direction in which the development of different types of regions might proceed in the future. The following sections will examine the results of the first phase of restructuring and will attempt to provide a picture of regional structures of Central Europe in the year 2005. Regional policies will also be discussed.

Social, Ethnic and Political Spatial Patterns

The historical processes have been responsible for creating, in Poland, a *nationally homogenous society*. Ethnic or national minorities constitute not more than 2 per cent of the Polish population. Such homogeneity was the result of World War II, during which almost the entire Jewish population had been exterminated and after which massive movements of population caused all other national minorities to leave the country (movement of frontiers to the west left the non-Polish population, who lived in the east of Poland, within the Soviet Union).

There are some ethnic differences within the Polish nation. Several ethnic groups (e.g. the highlanders, the Casubians, the Uppersilesians) do have their own traditions and cultures, demonstrated, among other manifestations, by their own dialects. However, the uniformisation principles – which have been the basic principles of the authoritarian regime – have eroded away much of the identity of these minorities.

Poland during its history has been a unitary state. With the exception of the period of feudal disintegration (12th–13th centuries) there has always been a central state power: the monarch, and from 1918 – state government (the strength of this authority was, however, another matter). In general, therefore, there is no tradition of regionalism or regional autonomy in Poland.

Regional differentiation of long-term economic development has produced marked differentiations of *social attitudes and skills*. In general, the Wielkopolska region should be considered as well advanced in self-organisation and entrepreneurial spirit. The same can be said of other societies in big urban centres, such as Warsaw, Kraków, Gdansk and Szczecin. On the opposite pole we find the societies of backward, rural regions in the east, though long-lasting traditions of local self-government, educational and cultural development positively distinguish the south eastern part of the country (Western Galicia). The population of the so-called 'regained territories' (the areas left by the Germans after World War II) have only recently acquired a level of social cohesion and have produced stronger social ties (in the main these territories were inhabited just after the war by Polish immigrants from the former eastern territories, lost to the Soviet Union).

There has been a long tradition of local *self-government* in Poland. Once again, Wielkopolska and Galicia should be considered as the leaders in this respect. However, due to the fact that the feudal system lasted in this country much longer than in Western Europe (serfdom was abolished as late as the 19th century), the self-governmental rights were restricted only to the gentry. The inter-war period brought the renaissance of local self-government in Poland, the under the socialist system local government was, in fact, emasculated and subordinated to the state authorities and to the communist party's local structures. It was only in 1990 that local self-government was restored to the whole country.

Regional policies have – even before the war – constituted an important part of the state development policy, at least in the official sphere. To some extent this was a bare historical necessity: twice this century Poland faced the tremendous task of *integrating the territory of the state* which had been composed of areas inherited from other countries. In 1918 Poland was made up of three parts which for almost a century and a half had been the peripheral regions of three states: Russia, Austria and Prussia. In 1945 Poland regained territories which for centuries had been under German domination. In both cases the integration of these territories was a very successful and fast process.

Already in the 1920s and especially in the 1930s Poland was one of the leaders of *modern regional policy* and two major projects: construction of the harbour in Gdynia and the already mentioned Central Industrial District were the most important manifestations of this experience. Before the war almost half of the Polish state's territory was subordinated to a kind of *regional planning*, which, at that time, was conducted in close co-ordination with general development planning (i.e. followed the principle of integrated planning).

The spatial dimension also achieved high importance in *socialist planning*. However, none of the goals formulated by the state authorities has been fully reached. In fact, the territorial system has been, throughout the entire period of socialist Poland, subordinated to the sectoral system – the region always losing to sectoral interests. As a result, further concentration of the economic and human potential proceeded and the hyper-concentrated Upper Silesia, which consumed up to one-quarter of the entire state investment in the post-war period, is the clearest example of this process.

Territorial Organisation

Three out of four countries in Central Europe are of similar size, Poland itself is 50 per cent greater than all three taken together. Table 2.1 presents basic data on their territories and their administrative organisation. The territorial organisation of the four states differs considerably. Polish regions (*voivodships*) are similar in size to Hungarian counties (*megye*) and both these units are larger than the Czech and Slovak districts. In all countries the government controls the tier(s) of territorial division above the local level.[1]

Table 2.1 Territorial and administrative structures in Central Europe

Countries	Total area 1000 km²	Number and status of administrative units		
		Regional	County\district	Local
Czech Republic	78.9	– 8 (1 urban) governmental abolished in 1991	75 (3 urban) governmental/ indirectly self-governmental	6237 self-governmental
Hungary	93.0	6 Representatives of the Republic (abolished in 1994)	19 governmental/ indirectly self-governmental, 20 towns of county status	2915 rural, 156 towns self-government
Poland	312.7	49 governmental/ indirectly self-governmental	267 purely governmental	2459 self-governmental
Slovakia	49.0	5 (2 urban) abolished in 1991	38 governmental	2679 rural, 135 towns, self-governmental

Source: Gorzelak *et al.* (1994)

---

1   These differences create some analytical problems. Only Hungarian and Polish administrative regions are comparable in size. Both Czech and Slovak districts are much smaller (and much more numerous) and the former regions (*kraje*) are bigger than the Hungarian counties and Polish voivodships. For clarity and synthetic presentation, the bigger Czech and Slovak units were used in all graphic presentations in this report.

The reforms which moved the East-Central European countries from the authoritarian rule to the democratic system have, paradoxically, led to increased centralisation on the territorial level.

In the first 'shock of freedom' the process of fragmentation of the territorial units took place in Czecho-Slovakia and Hungary. Hundreds (in the Czech Republic, over two thousand) of new municipalities were created, some of them not greater than 50 inhabitants. The regional level was abolished. In Hungary the attempts of creating big regions (governed by the so called 'Representatives of the Republic') were recently turned down by the left-liberal government. Also in Poland the peasant party, one of the two partners in the left-oriented coalition, has stopped the reforms which aimed at creating some 10 to 12 big regions.

As a result, in all Central European countries the self-government is limited to the very local level, composed of thousands of small municipalities (numbering up to over 6000 in the case of the Czech Republic). The regional level in all these countries is solely subordinated to the central government. The size of the regional units does not allow for any sensible own development policies of the regional administration, even if such a strange idea came to the minds of its representatives.

The self-governmental municipality seems to be the strongest in Poland both in terms of area and population – only 27 Polish communes have less than 2500 inhabitants. In Hungary one third of municipalities have a population smaller than 500 inhabitants. In the Czech Republic some 80 per cent of municipalities have a population of less than 1000. There are also differences in powers and functions of local governments. Polish municipalities seem to be the strongest economic and legal entities.

In all countries the capital cities have a decentralised power structure. Warsaw used to be divided into seven districts, each of them having the status of a 'normal' commune (though the biggest of them, Mokotów, inhabited by over 350,000 people, has a bigger population than several *voivodships*). The central Warsaw authority was relatively weak and there were no mechanism for efficiently managing the city as a whole. A similar situation exists in Budapest, which is composed of 22 districts with the central city authority has exactly the same status as any of the city districts.

It was only very recently when the administrative status of Warsaw changed. A big central municipality has been created, which is further subdivided into seven smaller subsidiary units. The central municipality is surrounded by several more peripheral units. The council of the central municipality elects the president of Warsaw. Initial assumptions that this reform would allow for greater efficiency of city management, since it was to strengthen the powers of the president and concentrated more territory (and therefore economic power) in the central district, have not materialised, however.

The discussed reforms of the territorial divisions of all four countries seem to be following the same path. The disputes conducted in every country lead to a conclusion that regions of the first order should be strengthened. Polish reform will probably result in creation of 12 to 14 such regions, although a figure of 25 has also been mentioned. It cannot be excluded that new six Hungarian regions will be created. Also in the Czech Republic it is claimed that a regional level, abolished in 1991, should be reintroduced.

References

Gorzelak, G., Kuklinski, A., Jalowiecki, B. and Zienkowski, L. (eds) (1994) 'Eastern and Central Europe 2000 – Final Report.' *Studies 2*. DGXII of the European Commission, Luxembourg.

Piskozub, A. (1987) *Dziedzicto Polskiej Przestrzeni* (The Heritage of the Polish Space). Warsawa-Wrocìaw-Kraków-Poxnan: Ossolineum.

CHAPTER 3

The Regional Patterns of Transformation

This chapter will discuss the statistical picture of the regional patterns of Polish reforms in a wider Central European context. It will present the regional differentiation of the demographic processes, the labour market (with special attention paid to unemployment), industrial restructuring, foreign capital and privatisation. It will also give account of the new regional structure of economic power. These are the main processes which are shaping the new economic geography of Poland and which create grounds for future regional structures.

Together with the beginning of transformation from a socialist to a capitalist system, Poland – like other Central European countries – became exposed to Western, capitalist forces and patterns of development. The socialist patterns of regional development, such as massive state-financed industrial investment, heavily subsidised housing, a voluntarist approach to land management and a stigma of 'non-productivity' attached to the social and even the technical infrastructure, have gone. Instead, the regions, in order to meet the challenges of international and domestic markets, have had to demonstrate a good natural and social environment, a highly skilled labour force, efficient production structures, the ability to innovate and to be richly equipped with modern infrastructure.

The heritage of history, coupled with the natural endowment of particular areas, have put particular regions of Central Europe in very different positions at their starting point for transformation. Only some of them appeared to be able to participate in creation of new economic and social structures. These are the *indisputable leaders of transformation*. On the other hand there is a group of regions which would not be able to compete successfully in the new international and national setting. In this way the *polarisation effect* has already manifested itself in the regional dimension of Central Europe, as in other – economic and social – dimensions.

The balance-sheet of regional potential for new conditions should therefore include the following items:

1. the settlement system;
2. quality of environment;

3. the quantitative and qualitative features of the labour market;

4. equipment with R&D centres;

5. equipment with infrastructure;

6. accessibility from international centres of innovation and capital.

We shall examine these below, paying most of our attention to Poland, but providing a wider Central European context when possible.

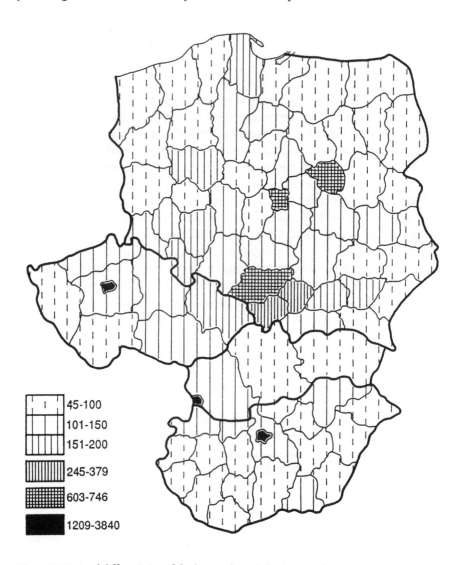

Figure 3.1 Regional differentiation of the density of population in Central Europe

Demography

Demographic processes are the least dynamic ones. It is only in times of massive migrations that the spatial structures of population change rapidly. Like other newly industrialised countries of Central and Eastern Europe, Poland has already gone through this period in the 1950s and the 1960s and – as explained below – in principle the stabilisation of the regional distribution of population has been achieved.

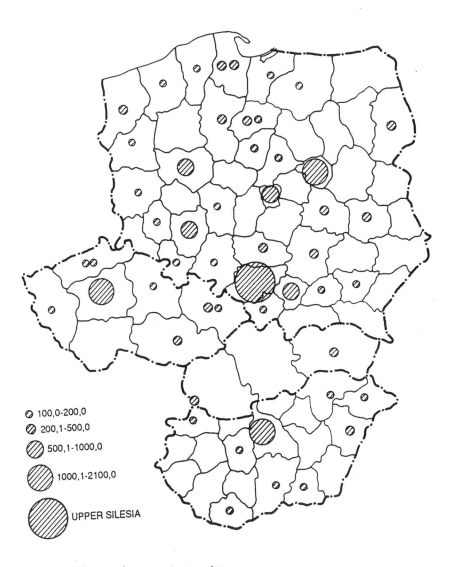

Figure 3.2 The biggest urban centres in Central Europe

Central Europe has a medium density of population, equal to 120 persons per 1 km². The Czech Republic is the most densely populated country (130 persons/km²), then comes Poland (122), Hungary (111) and Slovakia (108). Figure 3.1 presents the regional differentiation of density of population in Central Europe.

All four countries present a similar level of urbanisation (see Figure 3.2) 56 per cent of the Slovak, 62 per cent of the Hungarian and Polish population live in towns. In Poland the share of population living in towns of over 10,000 inhabitants equals 56.7 per cent and for the Czech Republic 55.7 per cent. In Poland the mostly urbanised regions in 1991 were the following: Lódz – 93.1 per cent, Warsaw – 88.8 per cent, Katowice – 87.2 per cent, Szczecin – 76.5 per cent, Gdansk – 76.2 per cent, Wroclaw – 74.2 per cent, Walbrzych – 74.0 per cent, Poznan – 71.3 per cent, and the least urbanised: Biala Podlaska – 36.5 per cent, Nowy Sacz –36.1 per cent, Tarnów – 36.0 per cent, Krosno – 35.3 per cent, Ostroleka – 34.7 per cent, Siedlce – 32.1 per cent, Zamosc –29.6 per cent, i.e. the regions of eastern and southern Poland.

The four Central European countries have reached *the stage of stability of their demographic and settlement systems*, though a constant, slow increase in the urban population can be observed.

The pace of change of the spatial structure of settlement has declined considerably in all four countries after the first stage of socialist industrialisation. The massive shift from the rural areas to towns ended somewhere in the 1960s, though in Slovakia it was prolonged to the 1970s. This slowdown of internal migrations was coupled with a fall in the birth rate. As a result, during the 1980s the regional dynamics of demographic processes were much lower then before.

The population of *Poland* is spread more or less evenly across its territory with only one – but important – exception for the Upper Silesia region. The Katowice voivodship (2.0% of the country's area) is inhabited by 10 per cent of the total population of Poland. The biggest town in Poland, Warsaw, has 1.7 million inhabitants (the metropolitan region of Warsaw hosts some 2.5 million), the second largest, Lódz, is approaching 1 million. The urban system is well developed and follows the rank-size rule, with four other big cities having a population above half a million (Gdansk-Gdynia-Sopot: 764,000; Kraków: 751,000; Poznan: 590,000; Wroclaw: 644,000).

Hungary is a clear example of a country dominated by one big urban agglomeration. Its capital, Budapest, inhabited by 2 million people, concentrates 20 per cent of the entire population of the country. No other town can compete with the role of the Hungarian capital – the next biggest towns with a population over 150,000 are the following: Debrecen (216,100), Miskolc (196,400), Szeged (177,700), Pécs (170,500).

The settlement structure of the *Czech and Slovak Republics* lies rather between the Polish and Hungarian structures. The two capitals – Prague and Bratislava – concentrate 11.8 per cent and 8.3 per cent of the overall population of these two new republics (their number of inhabitants is 1,215,000 and 441,500, respectively). In the Czech Republic, as in Hungary, the capital is by far the biggest city – the population of the next city, Brno, is close to 350,000. In the Slovak Republic only Kosice has reached the size of a larger city, with a population of 237,000. The cities next in terms of size (Nitra, Prešov, Banská Bystrica, Zilina) all have a population within the range of 80,000–90,000. In Slovakia there are only 10 towns with a population over 50,000 (in Poland there are 90 such towns, in Hungary 17 and in the Czech Republic 32).

The regional structures of the population and the settlement systems will not change to any significant extent in the coming years. The demographic processes described above will persist into the future.

However, the problem of *depopulating regions* which emerged recently will be even more acute for some areas. This will be the case in the Czech Republic (especially in northwest Bohemia, but also in northeast Bohemia) and in Hungary (the west of the country, though immigration may ease this problem there). In Poland some rural, northeastern areas may face demographic problems due to a distorted gender balance (a shortage of young women, who migrated to towns).

The overall increase of the Polish population during 1991 to 1994 amounted to 425,000, that is, 1.11 per cent. The highest demographic growth occurs in two groups of regions: the southeastern, with a large share of the rural population and northern and western parts of the country, with a younger population. Both these factors are responsible for a traditionally higher natural increase due to a high birth rate. There are two regions which have begun to decline in numbers – Lódz and Walbrzych – the two regions with particularly grave restructuring problems. The 1980s brought a deep decline (by 50%) of the traditionally high internal migrations, to some 500,000 per year. Even in Upper Silesia, which traditionally accommodated the highest numbers of newcomers, the positive migration balance became very small.

Warsaw kept its population stable. This region could have accommodated new in-comers and could have offered them jobs, which was not possible due to housing shortages.

The sex structure in several regions is seriously disturbed. In the north eastern parts of Poland for example, unmarried men outnumber unmarried women (in some localities this ratio may reach an extreme proportion of 7 to 1). Setting aside obvious social consequences, it gravely hampers agricultural output and, what is even more dangerous, clouds its future.

The regional distribution of Poland's population has been – in general – stable in the last few decades. During the 1990s there have been no major changes in the trends of the 1980s, when a drop in the spatial mobility of the population occurred. While in 1989 overall domestic migrations amounted to 596,500, in the next two years it dropped to 529,900 and 505,400, respectively (during the 1970s it exceeded 900,000 persons per annum). Net inflow into towns and cities during these three years was 139,800, 112,700 and 106,400.

New migratory patterns have emerged in some Polish regions. Upper Silesia is the most obvious example of this change. In the situation of a decrease of both inflow and outflow of people, the positive migration balance for the region became very small. It dropped from 27,000 in 1980 to a mere 2000 in 1992. Upper Silesia is no longer a region of opportunity. On the contrary it is now perceived to be a place which one should leave.

According to recent sociological surveys, half the people living there consider Upper Silesia as a relatively bad place to live, worse than other regions in Poland. More than one-third of people questioned declared that they were in a position to leave the region and almost half of them intended to do so. Around two-thirds of persons questioned would not seek the prosperity of their children or grandchildren in Upper Silesia and wished them to have an opportunity to emigrate from there.

Such attitudes may jeopardise the future educational composition of Upper Silesia. It is obvious that professionals and highly educated persons have better chances for moving, due to broader work opportunities and higher incomes. They are also more aware of the ecological situation of the region and, usually, are less attached to its traditions and cultural heritage. If these processes really take place, Upper Silesia's educational structure may further deteriorate, which could diminish its chances for successful restructuring.

During the 1980s the western territories of the *Czech Republic* have been losing their population at the rate of -4 to -2 per cent in a decade. The highest increase of the number of inhabitants, up to 10 per cent during the 1980s, was noted in the eastern and southwestern parts of the country (though the highest increase, of more than 10%, took place in the northern district of Ceska Lípa, the site of a uranium mine).

In *Hungary*, since the beginning of the 1980s, the total number of the population has declined rapidly, at a rate of -1.7 to -1.9 per cent per annum. The northeastern parts of the country noted the biggest growth in population. Heves, Hajdú-Bihar, Szaboles-Szamtár-Bereg – these are the regions with the youngest population. Demographic growth is also noted in some central (Fejér) and southwestern (Somogy) counties. The general tendency of migration from the east to the west is therefore natural and visible.

In *Slovakia* the fastest demographic growth takes place in the northern and eastern regions. Towns still gain in population, which does not seem to be the case in the other three countries (for example, during the 1980s Poprad increased its number of inhabitants by 39%, Banská Bystrica by 32%, Prešov by 28%). Only a few districts in the south have suffered a decrease in population.

This persisting decrease of domestic migration which emerged in all Central European countries during last decade reflects the decrease of real incomes and shortage of new housing. It leads to petrification of the regional structure of job opportunities. It is a kind of vicious circle: no 'working' labour market may be created without a sufficient supply of new housing and a propensity to migrate, which leads to slower economic growth even in the regions which could develop faster and which could accommodate new labour from areas of heavy unemployment. *Housing thus appears to be the crucial factor in the possible increase of internal migration and, in this way, achieving the adaptation of the spatial structure of the labour force to the spatially differentiated dynamics of economic development.* The situation in Poland in this respect is very typical of other Central European countries.

Housing for the entire post-war period was one of the most acute social and economic problems. There has always been a shortage of new dwellings, even in spite of the really great effort – at least in quantitative terms – to build more and more houses.

The rural areas were left to themselves. Only limited – in form of cheap loans – state support was available for the private farmers in their efforts to construct new dwellings and farm buildings. In towns the co-operatives, strictly subordinated to the state administration, constructed relatively cheap, by contemporary criteria, sub-standard, and heavily subsidised blocks of dwellings.

This situation changed dramatically. In fact, state support was withdrawn. The number of newly constructed dwellings dropped by 70 per cent, though some of them are now of a really high standard.

The most important changes took place in regulations relating to ownership of houses and dwellings. The restriction, according to which one household was allowed to own only one dwelling, was lifted. It opened the possibility of building houses for rent and of creating a more healthy market for houses and apartments. Though this did not solve the housing problem in Poland, it did create some hope that the construction sector would develop in the future, along with economic recovery and increase of incomes of population and domestic demand.

The regional differentiation of prices for apartments, houses and plots is a good indication of relative attractiveness of particular regions and towns. According to the most recent data, the price of $1m^2$ of an apartment in particular regions is the following:

'Prices of $1m^2$ in apartments, average prices, million zl				
		Number of rooms		
Total	1	2	3	4
Bialystok	4.7–4.9	4.5–5.1	4.5–4.9	4.4–4.6
Gdansk	5.0	5.0	4.6	5.0
Katowice	3.7	3.8	3.2–4.1	4.0
Kraków	6.0–7.0	6.0–6.5	6.0–6.5	5.5–6.0
Poznan	5.0–5.5	5.0–5.5	5.0–5.5	5.0–5.5
Szczecin	5.0–5.5	5.0–5.5	5.0–5.5	4.8–5.0
Warsaw	7.5–8.0	7.5–8.0	7.5–8.0	8.0–8.5
Wroclaw	4.8–5.3	4.8–5.3	4.8–5.3	4.8–5.3

Source: *Gazeta Wyborcza*, No 188, 13 August 1993, p. 14.

These are the average prices. The range may be much greater – for example, for a luxurious apartment in the 'best' part of Warsaw the price could be 18 million zl per $1m^2$ (some 1000 US dollars).

As can be seen, for one 4-room apartment in Warsaw one may buy two similar apartments in Katowice.

The age structure of the Polish population is much less regionally differentiated (Figures 3.3 and 3.4). The western and northern regions are demographically 'younger' – i.e. the shares of the pre-productive age groups are high and the shares of the post-productive age groups low. In the rural eastern and southern regions, the age structure of the population is the most polarised: high birth rates make the shares of the pre-productive age groups high, but also the shares of the post-productive age groups are the highest in the country. As a result, the urbanised regions have the highest shares of the productive age groups: (Katowice – 60.9%, Warsaw – 60.7%, Lódz – 60.0%, Szczecin – 59.8%, Wroclaw – 59.6%, Kraków – 59.3%, Opole – 59.3%, Legnica – 59.0%, and, on the other extreme, Ostroleka – 54.4%, Nowy Sacz – 54.1%, Chelm –54.0%, Przemysl – 53.9%, Zamosc – 53.3%, Siedlce – 53.3%, Lomza – 53.2%, Biala Podlaska – 52.9%).

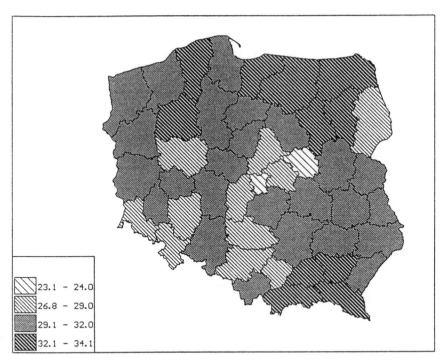

Figure 3.3 Share of population in pre-productive age in Poland, 1991

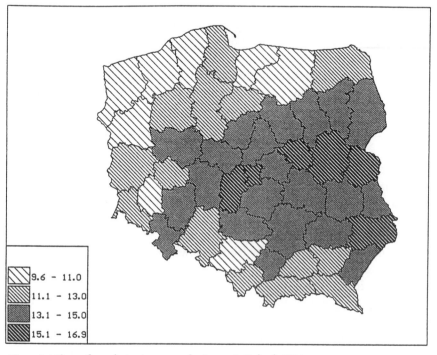

Figure 3.4 Share of population in post-productive age in Poland, 1991

The rents are regionally differentiated, too:

Monthly rents for apartments, average prices, million zl

	Number of rooms			
Town	1	2	3	4
Bialystok	1.3–1.5	1.6–1.8	2.0	2.0
Gdansk	1.8	2.0–2.5	2.5–3.0	3.0
Katowice	1.5	1.1–1.5	1.5–2.5	5.0
Kraków	1.5–2.0	2.5–3.5	3.0–3.5	3.5–4.0
Poznan	2.0–2.5	2.5–3.5	3.0–3.5	3.5–4.0
Szczecin	2.0–2.5	2.5–3.5	3.0–4.0	3.0–4.5
Warsaw	2.0–2.5	2.5–3.5	3.5–5.0	4.0–6.0
Wroclaw	1.5	2.0	2.5–3.0	3.5

Source: Gazeta Wyborcza, No 188, 13 August 1993, p. 14

These rents are much smaller – in relation to the average salary – than in the times when renting flats was illegal or semi-legal. Now, having a good salary, one may try to rent a flat and in this way adjust his/her place of living to the place of work. Once again, the pressure on the housing market in Katowice seems to be the lowest in the country, which is reflected by the low rents in this city (with the exception of the largest flats which are usually much bigger in this region than in other cities in Poland). Warsaw, as in the prices of flats, ranks on the first place.

One may easily envisage further development of the housing market in Poland and in this way growth of spatial mobility, first of highly paid specialists, then of wider strata of the population.

This pattern will be further reinforced by recent changes in the 'participation ratio', i.e. the share of population aged 15–64 in total population numbers. Due to the previous demographic processes, this ratio grows in the entire country, but the fastest growth occurs in northern and western regions. As it will be seen later, these regions have currently high unemployment rates. Demographic processes may therefore make the situation on the labour market even more difficult there.

The *international migrations* have not changed the basic settlement patterns of the four countries. It should also be expected that immigration from the East and emigration to the West will not pose dramatic problems for Central Europe. At the moment only very few Polish regions have lost population to Germany, but the scale of registered emigration is not in excess of 30,000 people per annum.

During the last few years this outflow has been constantly falling. According to the official statistics, which grasp only a small part of this phenomenon, the negative balance of external migration in last few years was as follows (in thousands): 1988, -34.2; 1989, -24.2; 1990, -15.8; 1991, -16.0. In this last year a considerable growth of the number of people coming to Poland occurred. In previous years this figure did not exceed 2600 persons, while in 1991 it jumped to 5000.

Since the beginning of the 1980s the health of Polish society deteriorated. The life expectancy for men dropped from 67.3 in 1975/76 to 66.7 in 1992. The abnormal mortality in the middle age brackets for men became the most visible manifestation of this process in Poland (for 1980 and 1992 respective values of male deaths per 1000 men in a given age bracket were the following: 45–54 years, 10.9 and 11.7; 55–59 years, 18.7 and 21.0; 60–64 years, 26.6 and 30.1).

A country is very often perceived through its capital. A great part of business contacts are concentrated in this particular city which usually – and this is the case in Central Europe – is the biggest city and the most important economic, cultural and political centre.

The *capitals* of the four Central European countries will assume the role of open European cities. There is a good chance that at least two of them – Budapest and Prague – will be able to join the second level of European metropoles and play the role of a gateway to Central Europe.

Prague, with its 1.3 million inhabitants by the year 2005, will regain its position as an international cultural and educational centre. This process has already started – in 1993 Prague hosted some 35,000 foreigners, mostly young people who enjoyed its rich cultural heritage, experimental spirit and intellectual atmosphere.

Budapest is very likely to become the commercial and financial centre of Central Europe. The development of business and financial services has been especially fast in this city after 1989. Budapest concentrates some 50–80 per cent of the national scientific and cultural potential, which places this city among the best equipped with an R&D base in the European metropoles of the second tier.

These two cities, Prague and Budapest, will have to solve their problems with a poorly maintained housing stock in their central areas and an obsolete urban infrastructure. The central districts of these cities will change their structure dramatically – from occupational functions to general business and cultural services. In the case of Prague the potential conflict between historic heritage and new service functions must be solved in favour of the historic urban structure, which is of a unique world-wide character.

Warsaw, located on the straight route from Paris and Berlin to Moscow and Kiev, seems to have the best position for becoming the gateway to the East and a meeting-point between the East and West. Being a relatively modern city (rebuilt almost completely after the World War II), Warsaw lacks the atmosphere of tradition and the flavour of history. On the other hand, it offers several excellent opportunities for locating new top quality services (hotels, banks, offices) in the very centre of the city. Creation of the CBD is still possible without the major cost of demolishing old structures. Relatively modern manufacturing and the presence of several high-quality R&D establishments are other important assets for Warsaw.

Bratislava seems to remain in the shadow of Vienna. This, however, may become one of the strongest assets of this city. Transfer of capital, contacts and know-how may be the most natural outcome of the proximity between the two cities.

The Regional Product

The regional product is the main synthesis-generating economic measure of the overall level of regional development. There are official statistics of the regional product in Poland (GDP in regional break-downs) for one year only, 1992 (see Zienkowski 1994).

The regional differentiation of GDP per inhabitant in 1992 and the share of agriculture are presented in Figures 3.5 and 3.6 respectively.

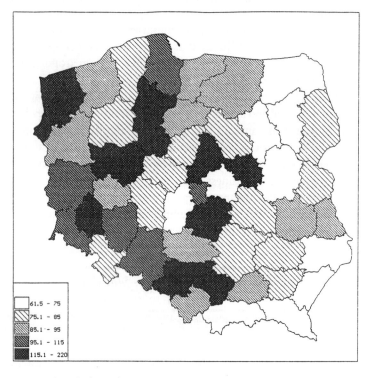

	61.5 - 75
	75.1 - 85
	85.1 - 95
	95.1 - 115
	115.1 - 220

Source: Zienkowski (1994)

Figure 3.5 Regional GDP per inhabitant in Poland in 1992, factor costs (national average = 100)

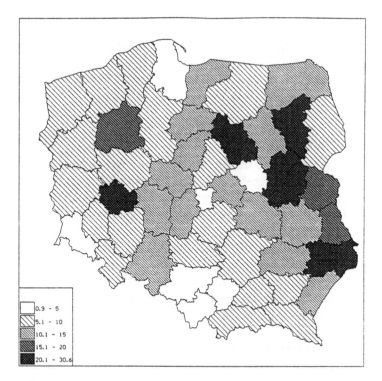

Source: Zienkowski (1994)

Figure 3.6 Share of agriculture in regional GDP creation, in Poland in 1991, factor costs

The big 'letter L' which begins in Gdansk and reaches the south-western corner of Poland to turn east and reach Kraków is clearly visible. This letter covers the regions of the highest level of development. Some other 'islands', for example Warsaw and Szczecin regions, may be added to this general pattern.

The regional discrepancies in the GDP per inhabitant level in Poland are now 2.5:1. This ratio should be regarded as very modest – in several West European countries, if they were to be divided to some 50 territorial units, this ratio would reach 4:1. Poland, as other post-socialist countries, appears to be a country with limited regional differences as expressed by the GDP. However, if the assumed rate of growth of the entire Polish economy is to reach 4.5–5 per cent per annum in the period until the year 2005, some regions will demonstrate much higher – and some much lower – rates of growth. The envisaged rates of growth of Polish regions are presented in Chapter 4.

The share of agriculture in GDP creation is strongly differentiated – from a mere 1.2 per cent in the Katowice region to over 20 per cent in several eastern and central parts of Poland. This figures reflect the regional differentiation of the economic structures in the country.

No estimates of the regional distribution of the GDP are available for other Central European countries.

The Labour Market

The changes in the labour market have become one of the most strongly pronounced effects of the post-socialist transformation. They can be treated, to some extent, as an indicator of the transformation processes, since the numbers and types of lost and newly created jobs precisely reflect more general economic processes.

This is true for both sides of the transformation processes. The overall recession manifested itself with different strengths in particular economic sectors – those hit most severely lost the greatest number of jobs. As a result, the regions in which these sectors used to play a dominant role, noted greatest redundancies and were affected by unemployment problems. Some sectors which experienced early recovery or have gone through a milder recession were able to defend their jobs.

The employment structures may also be examined from the point of view of the changes in the ownerships structure of the national economy. The changing shares of the public and private sectors represent the privatisation processes, which may be of double character. The growth of the share of the private sector (which was the case in Poland and in the majority of regions during 1989–1991) may not necessarily result from the real overall shift from the public to the private sector, but may be the outcome of a slower decrease in employment in the latter than in the former.

Employment

All Polish regions lost jobs during 1989–1991. In the northern and western voivodships this loss amounted to some 15 per cent of the numbers in work in 1989. This was mainly due to the collapse of state farms – for example, the loss of jobs in the public agricultural sector ranged in these regions from 50 per cent in Jelenia Góra to 32 per cent in Wroclaw (before 1990 state agriculture employed, in these regions, some 25–30% of the overall labour force active in agriculture and occupied over 50% of agricultural land).

Figure 3.7 presents the overall regional dynamics of the numbers working in the Polish economy during the period 1989–1991.

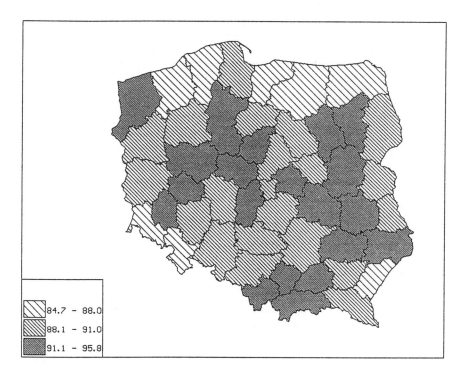

84.7 - 88.0
88.1 - 91.0
91.1 - 95.8

Figure 3.7 Dynamics of the number of working in the Polish economy, 1991 (1989 = 100)

No general spatial pattern can be seen. However, several observations can be made (they will be discussed in more detail below when the case studies are presented):

1. The regions in which state agriculture had employed the lion share of the agricultural population (northern and western parts of the country) noted the heaviest losses in employment.

2. The west-central part of the country (Wielkopolska) appeared to be the most resistant part of the country to the loss of employment.

3. The same situation occurred in the rural eastern regions.

4. Big urban-industrial centres behaved in an intermediate way or lost relatively few jobs.

Table 3.1 presents the beginning and end of arrangements of voivodships according to the dynamics of the total number in work during the period 1989–1991 in public and private sectors.

Table 3.1 Arrangements of Polish voivodships according to dynamics of the number of working, by type of ownership, 1989–1991

	Total			Public			Private	
No	Voivodship	1991 1989 = 100	No	Voivodship	1991 1989 = 100	No	Voivodship	1991 1989 = 100
1	Bydgoszcz	95.8	1	Siedlce	81.4	1	Szczecin	134.0
2	Siedlce	93.4	2	Tarnów	80.4	2	Bydgoszcz	128.0
3	Legnica	93.0	3	Legnica	80.2	3	Katowice	126.4
4	Skierniewice	92.9	4	Tarnobrzeg	78.8	4	Warsaw	126.0
5	Wloclawek	92.8	5	Piotrków	78.4	5	Poznan	126.0
6	Tarnów	92.8	6	Katowice	77.7	6	Lódz	123.3
7	Lublin	92.5	7	Bialystok	77.5	7	Gdansk	122.5
8	Kraków	92.5	8	Konin	77.2	8	Legnica	117.9
42	Przemysl	87.2	42	Szczecin	71.2	42	Bialystok	100.2
43	Olsztyn	86.2	43	Gdansk	70.8	43	Ciechannów	100.1
44	Slupsk	86.5	44	Krosno	70.6	44	Suwalki	99.3
45	Suwalki	86.4	45	Ciechanów	70.6	45	Zamosc	99.0
46	Elblag	86.4	46	Elblag	70.3	46	Siedlce	98.7
47	Jelenia Góra	85.1	47	Lódz	69.1	47	Biala Podlaska	98.5
48	Walbrzych	85.0	48	Warsaw	68.0	48	Przemysl	98.3
49	Koszalin	84.7	49	Poznan	65.6	49	Lomza	97.9

Source: own data and calculations

The shift from the public to the private sector took place mostly in the regions with big urban centres: Warsaw, Poznan, Lódz, Wroclaw, Kraków and Szczecin. These were the regions in which both the decrease of numbers in work in the public sector and the increase in the private sector were the greatest. In rural backward regions both sectors lost jobs.

This shift did not, however, follow a clear regional pattern, according to which the regions losing most of the jobs in the public sector would gain the most in the private one. The correlation coefficient between dynamics of the numbers working in both sectors during the period 1989–1991 was equal to only 0.42, i.e. it was not too high.

The growth of the number of those in work in the private economy was differentiated among particular sectors. Its regional/sectoral patterns are demonstrated in Table 3.2.

Table 3.2 Arrangements of Polish voivodships according to dynamics of the number of working in the private sphere, by sectors, 1989–1991

Industry				Construction				Domestic trade		
No	Voivodship	1991, 1989 = 100		No	Voivodship	1991 1989 = 100		No	Voivodship	1991 1989 = 100
1	Bydgoszcz	143.8		1	Szczecin	187.4		1	Lódz	204.2
2	Krosno	132.6		2	Opole	181.1		2	Warsaw	185.5
3	Torun	120.1		3	Katowice	176.2		3	Kraków	184.4
4	Poznan	188.7		4	Bielsko-Biala	175.2		4	Szczecin	176.4
5	Pila	117.8		5	Kraków	158.3		5	Poznan	171.2
6	Elblag	117.3		6	Legnica	157.1		6	Gdansk	170.7
7	Gdansk	114.7		7	Kalisz	155.1		7	Legnica	167.6
8	Katowice	113.9		8	Czestochowa	154.7		8	Lublin	42
42	Rzeszów	86.9		42	Przemysl	103.6		42	Kalisz	110.5
43	Siedlce	86.2		43	Zamosc	102.9		43	Bialystok	110.4
44	Jelenia Góra	84.6		44	Olsztyn	102.4		44	Zamosc	105.3
45	Lomza	84.1		45	Siedlce	100.0		45	Chelm	103.1
46	Czestochowa	83.5		46	Suwalki	97.8		46	Suwalki	102.9
47	Piotrków	81.1		47	Lomza	90.0		47	Biala Podlaska	101.1
48	Przemysl	80.4		48	Walbrzych	89.9		48	Lomza	100.0
49	Zamosc	69.9		49	Koszalin	84.3		49	Ciechanów	99.1

Source: own data and calculations

There is no general pattern of the regional dynamics of private employment in industry, though big urban centres demonstrate higher dynamics than rural areas. On the other hand, in such sectors as construction, and especially trade, the growth of the private sector was exceptionally high in the most urbanised voivodships.

The private sector was unable to create as many new jobs as have been shed in the public sector. Growth of *unemployment* was the direct effect of these (dis)proportions.

The educational level of the labour force

Until now we have spoken about the *quantitative* aspects of employment and the labour market. The *qualitative* aspect seems to be of no lesser importance in the changing economic world.

There were marked regional differences in respect of the professional skills of the labour force. The 'best' and the 'worst' regions are presented in Table 3.3.

Table 3.3 Economically active in Poland, by educational level, 1988

No	Voivodships	% with education	
		University and equivalent	Secondary
1.	Warsaw	19.7	40.7
2.	Kraków	14.1	28.9
3.	Wroclaw	13.4	32.8
4.	Poznan	12.5	30.4
5.	Lódz	12.3	36.0
6.	Gdansk	12.1	32.2
7.	Lublin	10.2	27.6
8.	Szczecin	10.1	30.8
9.	Olsztyn	8.6	29.4
10.	Koszalin	8.5	29.4
40.	Wloclawek	4.8	23.3
41.	Biala Podlaska	4.8	22.5
42.	Piotrków	4.7	22.4
43.	Konin	4.7	22.3
44.	Sieradz	4.4	19.7
45.	Ciechanów	4.3	24.1
46.	Lomza	4.3	20.7
47.	Zamosc	4.2	21.3
48.	Ostroleka	3.9	21.4
49.	Siedlce	3.9	19.7
	Poland	8.4	27.9

Source: Census data, Rocznik Statystyczny Województw 1990, Table 3(98)

Data quoted above are derived from the 1988 census. No more recent information of this type is available. However, not much could have changed during last six years and the structures presented here seem to be representative of the current state of regional differences in the educational level of the labour force.

As Table 3.3 demonstrates, in all big urban centres (with the exception of the Katowice region) the share of highly educated employees was higher than the national average. The backward agricultural regions occupy the opposite end of the table, being accompanied by the 'monofunctional' industrial centres which have their economic base in raw material extraction (Konin, Piotrków, Tarnobrzeg). For the biggest concentration of industrial employment in Poland, the Katowice region, the figures are 8.1 and 29.9 per cent, respectively. The Katowice region is the national leader in the share of the semi-secondary vocational (of a rather narrow profile) level of education. Of its active labour force 38.6 per cent (with 29.6% the national average and 20.6% for the Warsaw region) has attained this particular level, which, however, does not provide too many opportunities for efficient retraining and acquiring new skills.

There are therefore three major dimensions of the regional profiles of the educational level of the labour force:

- the 'big city' dimension;
- the rural dimension;
- the industrial dimension.

Warsaw, Kraków, Poznan, Wroclaw, Lódz and Gdansk fall into the first group. These regions are characterised by high shares of the labour force with university and secondary levels of education and relatively low levels of workers with semi-secondary vocational training.

Eastern and central regions constitute the 'rural' type of education, where all types of education are poorly represented and the share of the population with primary school level or even below that are the highest (up to 50% of the total numbers of the economically active; however, even in the Warsaw region every fifth person economically active has a primary or lower level of education – the national average is 34.1%).

The Katowice region is a typical example of the industrial type of education profile. Its shares of other types of education are close to the national average, which is much lower than it should have been taking into consideration the fact that this region has the biggest concentration of the urban population in Poland.

In the remaining three Central European countries all big cities also fall into the first group (see Figure 3.8). These regions are characterised by large shares of the labour force with university and secondary levels of education and relatively low levels of workers with semi-secondary vocational training. Similar to Warsaw, the share of university graduates in the over-25 population bracket in Prague approaches 20 per cent and in Budapest it exceeds 20 per cent (47% of all Hungarian college and university graduates work in the capital).

Similar to Poland, in rural peripheral regions this share may be as small as 4 per cent (in Polish and Slovak eastern regions). In Hungary the lowest rates of university education do not fall below 9 per cent and in the Czech Republic below 6 per cent.

The educational level of the labour force in industrial centres is, on average, not low. However, the educational structure has been subordinated to the requirements of industry. As a result, in such regions university education is biased towards engineering and the semi-skilled workers constitute the main group in the labour force. General secondary schooling and humanities are strongly underrepresented, which could hamper the possibilities for economic and social restructuring of such regions.

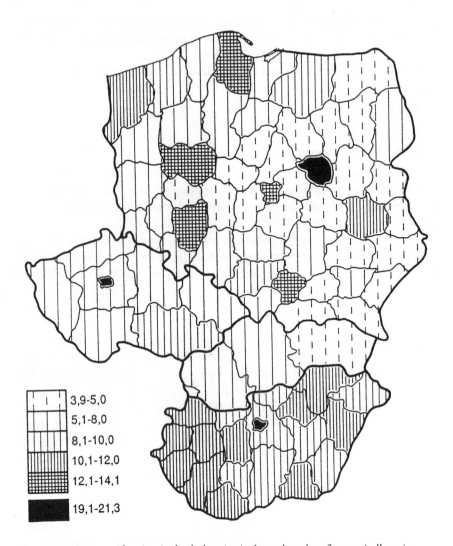

Figure 3.8 Percentage with university-level education in the total number of economically active,
*   Central Europe 1992*

The future situation of the regional labour markets in Central European countries
will be both a factor in and the result of restructuring and transformation. The
polarisation effect will be clearly pronounced during the next decade. The big
urban centres, already presenting the highest educational level of the labour force,
will tend to offer more educational opportunities. The backward rural areas will
be left behind and thus their development opportunities will be further hampered.

Such a regional distribution of the level of education of the labour force should
not be a surprise when considering the regional centres of higher education. Table

3.4 presents the major centres (excluding the military and police schools of university-level) in the academic years 1990/91 and 1992/93.

Table 3.4 Academic centres in Poland and employment in science

No	Main academic centres	Students 1990/ 1991	1992/ 1993	Academic teachers 1990/ 1991	1992/ 1993	Employed in science 1989	1992
1.	Warsaw	68.2	84.5	10.5	10.1	48.3	31.8
2.	Kraków	50.0	58.9	8.2	7.1	9.3	5.7
3.	Wroclaw	35.9	43.4	6.2	6.0	5.2	2.2
4.	Poznan	34.9	43.9	5.5	5.7	6.2	3.5
5.	Lublin	33.2	39.6	4.0	4.1	2.6	1.7
6.	Katowice[a]	32.7	43.6	5.3	5.1	12.7	8.4
7.	Gdansk[b]	25.6	28.7	5.4	3.9	3.6	2.5
8.	Lódz	22.9	28.9	4.7	4.6	8.8	3.7
9.	Szczecin	16.1	20.5	2.6	2.5	0.6	0.1
10.	Olsztyn	10.4	10.3	1.3	1.3	0.7	0.3
	Poland	403.8	495.7	64.5	63.1	115.4	70.2

Notes: [a]together with Gliwice Technical University; [b]together with High Maritime University in Gdynia

Sources: Rocznik Statystyczny (Statistical Yearbook) 1991, table 23(621), 5(100); 1993, table 24(624); *Rocznik Statystyczny Województw* 1993, table 2(101)

Warsaw in this field is a true national leader. It has 26 schools of university standard (out of 127 existing in Poland), out of which 7 are not subordinated to the government (there are 15 such schools altogether in Poland). Out of 7500 professors working in Polish universities and equivalent schools, 20 per cent of them work in Warsaw (shares for lower-level academic staff are lower for Warsaw). Of all Polish students 18 per cent conduct their studies in Warsaw. All university-level schools operating in Warsaw are high ranking among Polish establishments of university education. This may be proved by high efficiency in qualifying new staff for academic careers: one-third of all newly nominated professors, habilitated doctors and doctors work in Warsaw. This also means that academic establishments concentrated in Warsaw support other, weaker academic centres (also some foreign ones, due to a 10–15% 'brain-drain' from Polish science).

The effect of the brain drain (see Jalowiechi *et al.* 1992, 1994) is reflected in the heavy losses which Polish science suffered during the past years. In spite of the increase in the number of university students, the university staff was reduced (in fact, they left to other occupations in Poland and abroad). An even more dramatic situation occurred in non-academic employment in the R&D sector, which was deprived of almost 40 per cent of its 1989 employment. All regions lost scientific employment, though the Lódz voivodship was struck most severely.

Warsaw – as the national capital – hosts all decision-making bodies responsible for Polish science and academic life. It is the location of the headquarters of the Polish Academy of Sciences and the vast majority of its committees. Many institutes subordinated to particular ministries are also located in Warsaw.

Let us compare this domination by Warsaw with the situation in the Katowice region. In the Katowice voivodship there are only six schools at a university level (academies of economics, music and physical education, medical academy, poly-technic, and university). All these schools employ 700 full professors. The situation of several specialised institutes, which used to work for the needs of the industries concentrated in Upper Silesia, is very difficult. This is due to the bad situation these industries find themselves in, and their inability to commission research and to introduce new technologies. A great part of science of Upper Silesia will have to undergo deep restructuring, along with the industrial restructuring necessary in this region.

The domination of the capital cities in the educational systems of other Central European countries is also clearly visible. The regional differentiation of the scientific and academic potential is most pronounced in *Hungary*. *Budapest* hosts 70 per cent of all those employed in Hungarian R&D, 44 per cent of university and college students and 70 per cent of all PCs working in the country. There are 41 academic establishments in Budapest. It provides more than half the Hungarian patents (two-thirds of those registered abroad). Other academic centres in Hungary are of lesser relative significance (for example only one spatially spread institute – the Centre for Regional Studies – has its headquarters outside Budapest, in Pécs).

Prague hosts 5 out of 13 *Czech* academic institutions and most institutes of the Czech Academy of Sciences. Universities are also located at Brno (three universi-ties, several institutes), Plzen (one university, a few institutes), Ceské Budejovice (one college, a few institutes), Usti nad Labem (one college, a few institutes of applied research), Olomunc (one university with tradition), Ostrava (two universi-ties, several institutes of applied research).

In *Slovakia* over 55,000 students take their classes in 14 universities, and high schools operate in 10 locations. Obviously, Bratislava with its 5 universities and 24 faculties, is the national leader, hosting half of all Slovak students. Kosice comes second with three universities and almost 10,000 students. Nitra accommodates two universities, with over 5000 students.

For the overall spatial pattern of academic centres in Central Europe see Figure 3.9. The position of the traditional academic and scientific centres will not deteriorate in the future. This strong position is also manifested in international contacts of the most renowned academic establishments of Central Europe. It can be expected that the growth of outlays directed to higher education and science will be located in the already best and biggest centres, since they promise the most in terms of using these resources in the most efficient way. However, the increase of outlays spent on primary and secondary education should lead to more even regional distribution of basic educational opportunities and levelling of the quality of teaching.

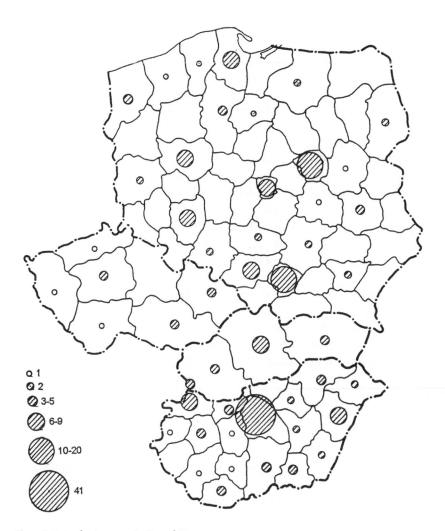

Figure 3.9 Academic centres in Central Europe

The emergence of professional training and retraining services will be the most pronounced phenomenon in the educational systems of the four countries. It can be expected that the old industrial regions will be the targets of these activities, since they need diversification of skills more than improvement of basic qualifications.

Statistical data prove without doubt that there is a negative relationship between the chance of being unemployed and the educational level. Only 2.4 per cent of the unemployed have university-level education, while as much as 37 per cent have semi-secondary vocational skills. These ratios differ considerably from the educational structure of those economically active. We shall discuss the problems of unemployment in the following section.

> The emergence of private and public professional training and retraining institutions (also targeted at the unemployed) is the only important change which has occurred recently. These offers are concentrated in big urban centres. The same applies to the participants of several distance education schools. For example, in the regional distribution of the students of one of the leading distance education schools based in Warsaw (with foreign capital involved), which offers courses in marketing, management, banking and foreign languages and which market its services in both local and national mass media, Warsaw is a clear leader with 16 per cent of all students. Other highly urbanised regions are also well represented (Katowice – 9%, Gdansk, Bydgoszcz, Lódz, Poznan, Szczecin, Wroclaw – each region providing some 4% of all students). This can be the result of several factors which are typical for great cities: greater awareness of the need of acquiring new skills; more job offers; wider distribution of newspapers and better developed reading habits; higher incomes (the prices of the courses are equal to 30–40% of the average wage) etc. Nevertheless, such new phenomena like training and retraining offers – even those which are not bound to the location of the school itself – further reinforce the uneven regional distribution of the educational level of the labour force, either by the fact that these offers are usually concentrated in big cities or by the response of the trainees themselves.

Unemployment

Unemployment is a genuinely new phenomenon in post-war Central Europe. Open unemployment did not exist prior to 1990 (though hidden unemployment – named by Kornai as 'unemployment on the job' (Kornai 1980), has been one of the strongest features of the socialist economy).

By the end of 1989 unemployment was virtually non-existent in Poland. Two years of transformation – 1990 and 1991 – each brought one million unemployed. By the end of 1993 there were 2,889,600 registered unemployed, 15.7 per cent of the economically active population and 25.2 per cent of those active outside private agriculture.[1] The rate of growth of this last indicator was faster than that

---

1   The rate of unemployment is defined as the relation of unemployed to the economically active population, i.e. to the total number of these at the productive age (women 18–59, men 18–64) who either work or express a wish to work.

of the total unemployment rate, which shows that the non-agricultural labour market is shrinking faster.

The dynamics of the growth of unemployment had a clear regional pattern. The northern regions of Poland were first to note massive unemployment, along with the collapse of the state farms. These regions have also noted higher than average growth of unemployment in 1993. As a result, these are the parts of Poland where unemployment is the highest and where opportunities for reversing this situation are rather bleak. In the regions of the northern belt the rate of unemployment exceeded 25 per cent (these are the following voivodships: Koszalin, Suwalki, Elblag, Olsztyn and Slupsk).

Two industrial regions, Lódz and Walbrzych, were the other classic regional examples of structural unemployment, which emerged on a massive scale in 1991. By the end of 1993 these two regions noted rates of unemployment of 20.4 per cent and 23.0 per cent respectively.

Highly urbanised regions, such as Warsaw, Poznan, Kraków and Katowice note the lowest unemployment rates, below 10 per cent. The reason for these relatively low figures are obvious in the first three cases – these regions present a diversified economic structure, which was relatively well adapted to the new economic conditions and which could cope with the transformation to a market economy relatively well. Low unemployment in the Katowice region is a result of the fact that a real restructuring of this region has not yet taken place, mainly due to the strong and defensive role of the trade unions.

The south eastern part of the country notes, on the average, relatively lower unemployment rates. To some extent this could be misleading, since in these regions there are several cases of single-industry 'company towns', i.e. towns which used to be dominated by one big industrial plant. The case of Starachowice, where unemployment now reaches 28.9,[2] will be recalled in the next section.[3] There are a few other such cases in this part of the country, like Mielec, Ostrowiec, Stalowa Wola – all these towns used to be dominated by one industrial plant which used to orient its production to the Eastern (Soviet) markets. The collapse of COMECON shaded the economic foundations of such localities and left their labour markets with massive unemployment.

Figure 3.10 presents the most recent available regional differentiation of the unemployment rate in 49 administrative Polish regions (voivodships). The spatial differentiation presented does not provide a full picture of unemployment in Poland. It is obvious that in several localities this phenomenon is even more dramatic than can be seen in the 'averaged' picture. The differentiation of the rates

---

2   This figure relates to the so-called 'employment region' of Starachowice. There are 355 such regions, composed of communes and towns and not crossing the voivodship boundaries, which were created by the Ministry of Labour and Social Policy to cope with the local Labour markets, and especially with unemployment.
3   See also A. Robinson (1994).

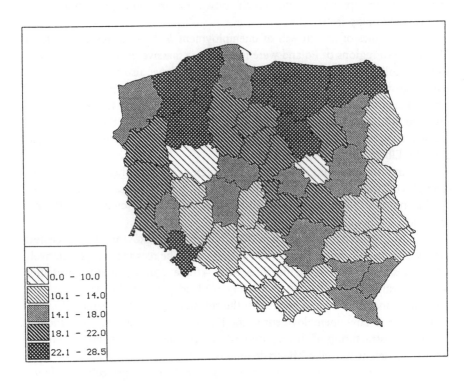

Figure 3.10 Unemployment rates by Polish regions, April 1994

of unemployment is much greater on the level of the 355 employment micro-regions. The range of this rate extends from 4 per cent in the Bialobrzegi micro-region (central Poland) to 42.6 per cent in the Paslek micro-region (in the Elblag voivodship). This range keeps expanding, which shows growing differences in the regional and local potentials for transformation. There are areas where the number of unemployed exceeds even by 50 per cent the number of those who have work. Several localities have been left almost without any economic base, since a dominating factory or state agricultural farm has collapsed (some of such cases will be discussed in the later parts of this report). Especially dramatic situations occur in remote underdeveloped rural areas where job opportunities are virtually non-existent.

The number of unemployed persons should be related to the number of jobs on offer. Table 3.5 presents these figures for selected regions.

The pattern is evident: all big cities (with the exception of Lódz) are, relatively, in a better situation, though 50 or 70 unemployed persons per one job offer cannot be, in any case, considered as a feature of a good labour market. The Lódz region, with its 192 unemployed per one job offer, places it alongside the backward rural regions of the east and the northern part of Poland, where state agriculture shed most of its employment.

Table 3.5 Relation of registered unemployed to jobs on offer in Poland, June 1992, by regions

No	Voivodships	Unemployed per 1 job on offer
1	Warsaw	12
2	Gdansk	22
3	Leszno	33
4	Poznan	33
5	Gorzów	35
6	Katowice	40
7	Radom	46
8	Szczecin	48
9	Wroclaw	52
10	Konin	52
40	Otroieka	249
41	Rzeszów	252
42	Chelm	257
43	Elblag	258
44	Pila	271
45	Zamosc	381
46	Walbrzych	400
47	Suwalki	421
48	Ciechanów	536
49	Lomza	586

Source: Central Statistical Office 1992, table 27

In the other two countries: Hungary and Slovakia *unemployment* became one of the most pronounced outcomes of the transformation. In the Czech Republic this phenomenon virtually does not exist yet, since the restructuring process has been delayed in this country due to the adopted strategy of economic transformation. To some extent the 'Czech pattern' may be applied to Polish Upper Silesia, where, due to socio-political reasons, restructuring has been delayed and unemployment did not manifest itself in the same strength as if it had happened in the case of restructuring similar to other industries and regions.

Figure 3.11 presents the regional distribution of unemployment in the four Central European countries.

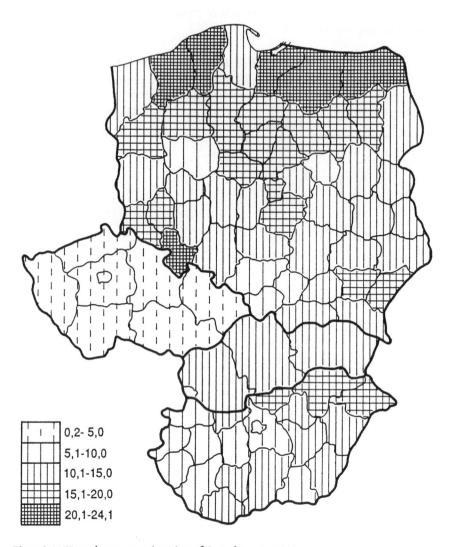

| | | 0,2- 5,0 |
| 5,1-10,0 |
| 10,1-15,0 |
| 15,1-20,0 |
| 20,1-24,1 |

Figure 3.11 Unemployment rates in regions of Central Europe, 1992

There have been different reasons for the emergence of mass unemployment in Central Europe. Losing the 'rouble markets' of the former COMECON countries was one of the most important, especially in the case of single-industry towns. This was the case in south eastern Poland, north western Hungary, and the eastern part of the Eastern Bohemia region in the Czech Republic. Inability to sustain competition of more effective Western supplies was another reason for the collapse of several manufacturing industries, sometimes advanced technologically. Restructuring of agriculture is another cause of unemployment. Since it occurs in predominantly rural areas which do not offer other job opportunities, this factor causes the most grave structural unemployment.

It has been commonly accepted that unemployment in the *Czech Republic* was almost certain to occur in the future. It was argued – basing on the experience of other post-socialist countries – that it is impossible to restructure the economy without encountering sharp problems on the labour market. These opinions have not materialised as fact. The Czechs seem to succeed in economic reforms without running into severe problems on their labour market although some reforms may go through some tension. In fact, unemployment in the Czech republic almost does not exist (being equal to 3–4%) and in the city of Prague, with unemployment equal to 0.2%, the situation resembles socialist times, where labour was in acute shortage. Only in *North Moravia* is unemployment approaching 5% considered a serious problem because of the difficulties of the textile and electrical industries.

The experiences of the Ostrava-Karviná region shed some light onto the restructuring of the regions dominated by the heavy industry (see Nesporova and Kyloh 1994). The region supplies 90 per cent of coal and steel produced in the republic. Since 1989 it was known that the profile of the region cannot be maintained forever and that deep changes in its economy must occur. State subsidies and investment were sharply decreased. However, the devaluation of the national currency made the production of the region competitive on the Western markets and able to replace the supplies form Poland and Ukraine, thus prolonging the profitability of the two leading branches. As a result, the restructuring has not been profound and has not lead to dramatic social costs and tensions. However, the situation in this region may still worsen dramatically, following the expected restructuring of the heavy industries concentrated there, and the spin-offs from the envisaged restructuring may also strike the neighbouring districts of Novy Icín and Opava. Unemployment may also rise in the nearby Vsetín district due to the decline of the electrical industry.

In *Hungary* a clear division of the country into three parts can be seen: Budapest, with the lowest rates of unemployment (ca 5%); the western part, with unemployment at around 10 per cent; and the east, where the rate may exceed 20 per cent. Such a distribution of unemployment follows the reactions of particular regional economies to the restructuring processes. Problems of the mining and metallurgy sectors are concentrated in the north (Borsod-Abúj-Zemplén county), centre (near Székesfehérván, south west of Budapest) and it is expected in the South near Pécs. The collapse of socialised agriculture was the main factor affecting job losses in the backward east.

In *Slovakia* the industrial restructuring seems to be deepest and the most painful of the four countries, thus leading to the most pronounced difficulties on the labour market. A pattern of 'internal colonisation' which was adopted within the former Czechoslovakia has left the Slovak territories with heavy and military industries (especially in Central Slovakia) which cannot find demand for their products. In several districts unemployment rates exceed 20 per cent. This is the case with the belt of the most peripheral border regions of the southern and eastern parts of country, though high unemployment also exists in some northern districts (in this last case the loss of jobs in northern Moravia, now the part of the Czech Republic, added to the difficulties on the local labour markets). Only Bratislava and Kosice can defend their labour markets, though expected problems with iron works in Kosice may worsen this situation soon.

In all four countries some of the jobs lost in the state-owned sectors were regained due to the development of the *private sector*. The development of privately owned firms was not evenly distributed regionally. In all four countries the biggest urban centres concentrated the fastest development of the private sector, mostly in trade, business services and manufacturing. In the eastern parts privatisation was much slower. Agriculture seems to be the economic sector most resistant to privatisation, which adds to the problems of local and regional labour markets of peripheral agricultural regions in all countries.

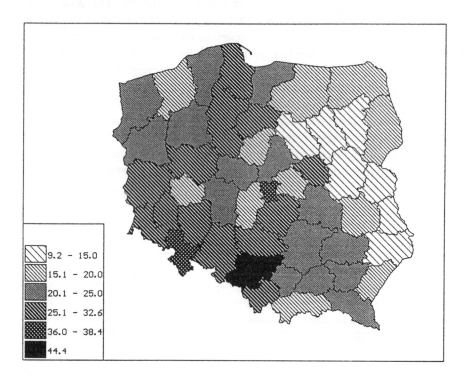

Figure 3.12 Share of working in Polish industry in the total number of working, 1991

Economic Restructuring

Industrial restructuring

According to the urbanisation-industrialisation-welfare pattern, big Polish urban centres are also the industrial centres (see Figure 3.12 for shares of industry in the total labour force in Poland). New processes have not changed this general pattern, on the contrary, industrial restructuring brought even greater concentration of industrial production in the leading regions.

Table 3.6 presents the shares of the strongest regions in the total industrial production of Poland. The cumulated share of the first 12 voivodships in national industrial production grew from 58 per cent in 1989 to 62.5 per cent in 1992. The share of the 12 least industrialised regions was stable at 5 per cent.

Table 3.6 Shares of leading Polish regions in industrial production, current prices (1989: socialised sector only)

Regions	1989	1990	1991	1992
Katowice	15.5	16.9	17.8	17.3
Warsaw	7.8	7.8	7.8	9.3
Lódz	4.3	3.7	3.4	2.9
Kraków	3.9	4.2	3.9	4.1
Gdansk	3.8	3.9	4.3	5.0
Poznan	3.7	3.9	4.4	4.4
Bielsko-Biala	3.5	3.2	3.1	3.3
Wroclaw	3.4	3.1	3.0	2.6
Plock	3.2	3.7	3.6	4.9
Bydgoszcz	3.2	3.0	3.3	3.4
Szczecin	2.9	2.8	2.6	3.1
Opole	2.8	2.9	2.8	2.2
Legnica	2.7	3.6	3.1	2.1

Source: Central Planning Office April 1993

The restructuring processes have taken place in several branches of Polish industry. In many cases these have mainly been 'negative restructuring', i.e. the process of curtailing several directions of production and closing down factories, almost entirely in the public sector. The reactions of particular industrial branches to the new economic conditions were presented in the previous chapter.

Particular industrial branches have diverged in terms of performance. In general, most of them have been through deep decline in 1990 and 1991. In 1992 this situation changed dramatically. Traditional branches of heavy industry have still been in deep decline, while consumer-oriented branches showed substantial growth in 1992. These processes have also persisted in 1993 and 1994, when the mining and the heavy industries sunk in recession and several manufacturing branches maintained their accelerated growth of up to 10–12 per cent of sales. It can be easily foreseen that these tendencies will persist into the future and that they will impact on the performance of particular regions.

Regional differences in *labour productivity* can be considered as the most meaningful indicator of the changes in regional economic structures. This indicator, however, is sensitive to several processes and phenomena. The two most important ones are the regional structures themselves and their dynamics, and the dynamics of price relations. The joint effect of both these processes may be said to reflect the regions' economic potential and their reaction to the changing economic environment.

Table 3.7 presents the changes in voivodships' positions in terms of labour productivity in industry. The first and last eight voivodships in 1991 are shown and the changes in their placing in comparison to the arrangement for 1990 is indicated. Though Table 3.7 provides a fragmentary picture, several observations can be made.

Table 3.7 Arrangements of Polish voivodships according to labour productivity in industry in 1991 and change of places in comparison with 1990

	Total			Public			Private	
No	Voivodship	Change	No	Voivodship	Change	No	Voivodship	Change
1	Plock	0	1	Plock	0	1	Lomza	+2
2	Warsaw	+1	2	Warsaw	0	2	Torun	0
3	Gdansk	+5	3	Kraków	0	3	Ostroleka	+26
4	Kraków	0	4	Gdansk	+4	4	Szczecin	0
5	Szczecin	0	5	Ostroleka	+6	5	Elblag	+12
6	Ostroleka	+12	6	Szczecin	-2	6	Koszalin	-1
7	Konin	+3	7	Konin	+6	7	Leszno	+8
8	Elblag	+13	8	Wloclawek	+1	8	Gdansk	+5
42	Nowy Sacz	+5	42	Lódz	+3	42	Kalisz	+5
43	Legnica	-41	43	Legnica	-38	43	Zamosc	-1
44	Chelm	-21	44	Chelm	-23	44	Lódz	-12
45	Walbrzych	-1	45	Walbrzych	+1	45	Czestochowa	+1
46	Lódz	-1	46	Pila	-10	46	Rzeszów	-3
47	Biala Podlaska	+1	47	Kalisz	-8	47	Krosno	-2
48	Kalisz	-6	48	Kielce	-6	48	Przemysl	-2
49	Kielce	-9	49	Biala Podlaska	-2	49	Tarnobrzeg	0

Source: own data and calculations.

First, it shows the regions with the highest productivity in industry: Plock (oil refinery), Warsaw, Gdansk, Kraków, Szczecin (diversified industry); and with the lowest, among which we find the two regions demanding heavy restructuring: Lódz and Walbrzych. Correlation between labour productivity in industry in the public sector and the regional GDP is significantly positive, though not very high (0.47). The case of Lódz is especially instructive from the point of view of internal consistency of low productivity in both public and private sectors.

Second, the table demonstrates how unstable the situation in industry was at the beginning of the restructuring process. Several voivodships have changed their position dramatically (some of the cases are not presented in Table 3.7 – for example the Skierniewice voivodship noted the highest productivity in private industry in 1990, but in 1991 it came only 22nd). Changes in the relations of prices, the collapse of one big enterprise or putting into motion a new establishment (especially in a less industrialised region) may change the relative position of a region from the very best to the very worst.

Third, the table demonstrates the differences between the regional patterns of labour productivity in private and public industry (the correlation coefficient between these two variables for 1991 was equal to zero). It is impossible to evaluate how the informalities, tax offenses etc., so common in private business in Poland these days, have impacted on that. On the other hand one cannot rule out the possibility that the private sector in Poland is beginning to establish new patterns of regional efficiency and productivity.

Restructuring of local systems: case studies

There are several typical cases of economic restructuring. The following section will give account of some of them in Poland and other Central European countries.[4]

Lubawka, a town and adjacent commune in the south western corner of Poland, presents much greater – though still distant in time – chances for re-development. Currently this local system is in a very difficult situation, since its main industrial enterprises have collapsed (PHARE Programme for Local Initiatives coordinated by the textile factory, which used to employ 1264 persons, has shed all of its employees by 1 June 1993; an asbestos plant will be partly closed in the near future due to ecological reasons; several other firms have losses and are at the edge of bankruptcy); this situation is further aggravated by the collapse of state-owned farms.

---

4   The first three case studies were based on the documents of the PHARE Programme for Local Initiatives coordinated by the Co-operation Fund.

The border crossing to the Czech Republic is the major chance for this particular locality. At present, this crossing is more of a local character. However, one of the major highways (see p.105) will pass through Lubawka. Survival to the moment when this highway is constructed and the major frontier point is opened will be the main problem for this locality in the coming years. Will it be able to sustain current difficulties and preserve some human and economic potential to meet this chance?

Dzialdowo presents still another type of a local problem. This is a town located in mid-eastern Poland, some 200 kms north of Warsaw. After four centuries of belonging to Prussia it came back after World War I to Poland. The population of the town and adjacent commune amounts to some 30,000 persons. It used to be a locality which based its economy on two sectors: agriculture and transport – Dzialdowo is a major railway node. The collapse of the state-owned farm, which owned more than half of all agricultural land in the commune, resulted in leaving 800 persons without work and further 200 jobs are to go in the near future. In the town Dzialdowo there are 2500 unemployed and the unemployment ratio reaches 25 per cent.

The commune Dzialdowo used to be a locality 'run' by the state-owned farm – almost like Starachowice used to be a 'company-town' which was developed by the truck factory. As in Starachowice, the collapse of the state farm left the commune without its economic base and without the sole supporter of its infrastructure. No other work opportunities are available, since town and commune Dzialdowo are surrounded by localities in a similar situation. Private farmers have no interest buying land left idle by the former owner, due to the low profitability of agricultural production and lack a of capital.

Dzialdowo may have its chance in developing a diversified industrial structure. Some examples of involvement of foreign capital have already emerged: German capital owns 75 per cent of the glass factory, which has a 20 per cent share on the German market. The location advantages on the crossing of major railways are the best opportunity for Dzialdowo and this asset should be developed at the first priority.

Starachowice is a 60,000 town in south eastern Poland. It is the third biggest town of the Kielce voivodship. Since ancient times iron production used to be the main direction of economic activity. The programme of the Central Industrial District, a major industrial understanding in Poland in the 1930s, related to these traditions. Starachowice became one of the centres of the entire undertaking. During the post-war period a major investment – a truck factory – was located in the town and soon it became the sole development factor of this medium-sized urban system.

In the 1970 there were 26,000 trucks produced yearly and the maximum employment reached 14,000 (half of all working in the town). Since the end of 1980 the truck factory entered a deep decline and there are no chances of coming back to the previous prosperity. The yearly production has been constantly dropping: 6000 trucks in 1990, 2400 in 1991, 1600 in 1992. Employment declined at a slightly slower pace: 6600 in 1990, 4700 in 1991, 4300 in 1992 (in mid-1993 employment equalled 4200 people). Overmanning is therefore the next problem for the factory management (it is estimated at some 20–80%, depending on the plant and type of work).

Competition of much better and – if bought second-hand – also cheaper trucks from the West was the main reason for this decline. Also the shrinking demand of the army added to these difficulties.

This situation can hardly be solved. It is doubtful that a serious Western truck-producer would seek contacts with the Starachowice factory. It does not have sufficient funds (it is even seriously indebted to the banks, to the state and municipal budgets and to its suppliers) to undertake designing and preparatory works to propose a new competitive model of a truck.

This hopeless situation of the factory also makes the situation of the town very difficult. The factory was not only the main employer for the town and the adjacent communes, but was also the owner or the founder of the main part of town social and technical infrastructure. The collapse of the factory (accompanied by the difficulties of other industrial firms located in Starachowice) in all dimensions also means the collapse of the town.

There are 6500 unemployed in Starachowice and the unemployment rate reaches 25.3 per cent. These rates are even higher in adjacent rural areas, up to 40 per cent for the non-agricultural population in one of them. The graduates of the narrowly profiled semi-secondary vocational schools (the schools were run by the factory and prepared young men for becoming its workers) constitute almost 40 per cent of all unemployed in Starachowice.

The labour market of Starachowice cannot be healed even by a very active and efficient approach from local authorities and governmental services responsible for coping with unemployment. As a result of these activities 1200 persons obtained temporary jobs at the 'intervention works' and 69 permanent jobs were created; almost 700 unemployed were involved in public works; 96 persons were retrained; 383 jobs were created with the assistance of credits directed to firms employing unemployed and the unemployed themselves; 74 persons were employed in infrastructure projects, financed by grants from the government. In spite of all these initiatives the local labour market will be crippled for several years.

Starachowice is a typical example of a company-town of south eastern Poland. Almost the entire area of the Central Industrial District is in similar difficult situation. This was one of the main suppliers of specialised machinery, to a large extent subordinated to the specialisation directions adopted within COMECOM and then located on the eastern markets. This region has been struck by the collapse of the Soviet empire especially strongly. The chances of its revitalisation are bleak, mostly due to location disadvantages and to a relatively poorly developed infrastructure. Moreover, the educational profile of the labour force was shaped by the needs of the industry and retraining is rather difficult.

These three examples illustrate very well the different types of local economic restructuring in Poland. They prove how difficult a local economic – and therefore also social – situation is faced and to what extent the chances for its improvement lie outside a given local system (see the next box).[5]

The case of the 'Tourist Six' municipalities located in the south western part of Poland may be recalled to illustrate the development of a local system based on its own potential.

Five of these municipalities are crossed by the international road E–67 Prague–Wroclaw. One of the most busy Polish border crossings, capturing most of the traffic from south western Europe, is located on the Polish–Czech frontier in Slone, in the Kudowa municipality.

The area forms a natural environmental entity. Natural conditions favour health services, recreation and winter sports. Snow may last till April and on the northern slopes even till early July. The climate is relatively mild for highlands which is the result of the oceanic influences of the Atlantic. The shrine of Wambierzyce – a pilgrim place – attracts several thousands of visitors yearly. Moreover, the area has long traditions of hosting visitors and tourists.

No other local economic sector can compete with tourism, especially in a situation when all other economic sectors of the locality are in a deep decline. The glass factories undergo deep restructuring, the plant producing electrical equipment for cars is in decline, the textile factories have lost their market and have shed jobs etc.

---

5   Gieorgica, Gorzelak and Jalowiecki 1992.

The tourist sector itself must undergo deep restructuring, too. In opposition to industry, this restructuring has good chances for final success. The state tourist sector has collapsed almost entirely. It had been heavily subsidised and when subsidies were withdrawn the demand shrunk dramatically. The private sector is developing but is still weak both in terms of material structure and professionalism. Education and diffusion of positive examples appear to be the most efficient method of enhancing local potential of the private tourist sector.

In response to these chances and challenges, all six municipalities created an inter-municipal association, Consortium 'Tourist Six', a public body. The municipalities have input initial capital. The activities of the consortium have already led to the collection of several grants and getting logistic assistance from several institutions and state agencies. Foreign contacts have been established, which will help a broader promotion of the region and its tourist services. In the next tourist season the consortium will act as the local 'manager' and promoter of the main part of the local tourist system. This example has also been publicised among other tourist regions and localities in Poland which will use the positive experience in developing their tourist activities.

It should be noted that the 'Tourist Six' is, formally, a part of the deeply depressed old industrial region – the Walbrzych voivodship. In the 'Tourist Six' itself, the unemployment rate reached 15–16 per cent. This example demonstrates, however, that within larger spatial settings which are generally labelled as declining or needing assistance there may be 'enclaves' of chances and local potentialities which may be developed by the activity of local authorities and the representatives of the local private sector. The positive role of new institutions is the best lesson of the 'Tourist Six'.

Privatisation

As a result of the privatisation processes (and also as an outcome of the collapse of several state-owned firms), by the end of 1992 over 50 per cent of the economically active population are working in the private sphere, out of which approximately half are outside agriculture. Several branches, like services and trade, have been privatised almost entirely.

As in other processes of transformation, the regional differentiation of privatisation is great. Figure 3.13 presents the regional patterns of 'capital' privatisation (see p.23) in Poland. Two main spatial factors seem to have shaped the regional differentiation of the privatisation process in Poland: the division into western and eastern parts of the country and the level of urbanisation. As in several other processes, the fastest pace of privatisation occurs in highly industrialised and urbanised regions.

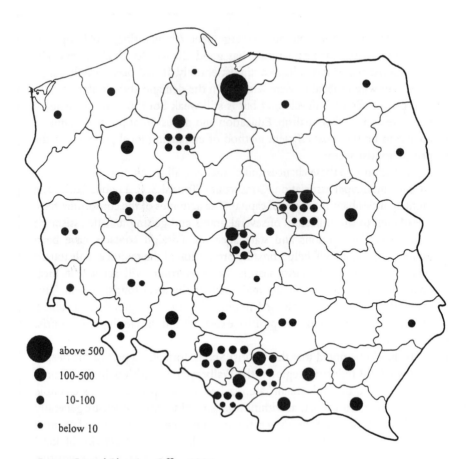

above 500

100-500

10-100

below 10

Source: Central Planning Office 1994

Figure 3.13 Privatised enterprises in the capital way and their value in bln zl, June 1993

In effect, the structure of both production and employment by sectors is changing. In the following voivodships the decrease of the share of the public sector in total employment was the fastest during 1989–1991 (in percentage points): Poznan, -16.1; Warsaw, -15.2; Szczecin, -15.1; Lódz, -14.1; Bydgoszcz, -13.8; Gdansk, -13.4; Zielona Góra, -11.5; Elblag, - 10.6; on the other side are the eastern and central regions, where this change of ownership structures was the slowest: Radom, -6.2; Bialystok, -6.2; Tarnobrzeg, -6.1; Biala Podlaska, -5.9; Tarnów, -5.6; Zamosc, -5.3; Lomza, -5.0; Siedlce, -4.0.

The deepest changes in ownership structure, represented by the differences of shares of employment in the public sector between the years 1989 and 1991, took place in the most urbanised and highly developed regions. On the other side of the spectrum of this divide are the rural peripheral voivodships in which this share dropped by only some 5–6 percentage points.

The most dynamic changes in ownership structures took place in the domestic trade, the most 'natural' sector to be privatised (it is composed of small establishments which need massive capital input). Once again, the 'city-regions' were the fastest in the privatisation process. The following voivodships were the fastest to privatise this economic sector (in percentage points of decrease in the share of the public sector during 1989 and 1991): Lódz, -27.2; Warsaw, -24.8; Gdansk, -23.2; Kraków, - 22.2; Szczecin, -21.3; Katowice, -21.1; Poznan, -19.4; Lublin, - 18.9; Wroclaw, -18.2; Bydgoszcz, -16.5. The slowest were the following regions: Przemysl, -10.8; Tarnów, -10.7; Tarnobrzeg, - 10.6; Siedlce, -10.4; Krosno, -10.4; Nowy Sacz, -10.2; Wloclawek, -10.2; Kielce, -9.3; Radom, -9.0; Plock, -8.5; Sieradz, -8.3; Chelm, -7.8; Ostroleka, -7.3; Ciechanów, -7.2; Lomza, -5.9; Kalisz, -5.6; Biala Podlaska, -5.1; Zamosc, -4.0. The vast majority of these regions are located in the eastern and central parts of the country.

There are several concentrations of private business in Poland – usually in the vicinity of big cities. The private business belts around Warsaw and Poznan have developed even in the 1970s and have maintained their exceptional economic structure in the 1990s.

The commune of Lomianki, just north west of the city of Warsaw, may be one of the best examples of such cases. Its population (town and adjacent commune) equals to 14,000. There are 85 ltd companies; two-thirds of them being small, since they employ up to five persons. Moreover, there are 550 firms owned by physical persons and further 132 personal companies. Most of them operate in manufacturing and in commerce. This high activity of the private sector in Lomianki is reflected in accelerated development of housing and the social and technical infrastructure and, moreover, has easy access to the facilities offered by nearby Warsaw. Lomianki is by far the richest municipality in Poland, since the revenues of the municipal budget are in the main part constituted by taxes and fees paid by private entrepreneurs.

However, as these entrepreneurs claim, the 'golden era' of their businesses is over. The unsatisfied market of the former socialist system offered the best conditions for their operations. Everything that was produced could easily find demand, which is not the case nowadays, when the market is limited on the demand side and when competition from abroad has a great share of all purchases.

It can be seen, though, that the localities which have long traditions of private business, which are well equipped with municipal and technical infrastructure and which are located close to the big markets of large urban centres, have far better chances for adapting to new conditions. The Lomianki municipality no doubt will survive the worse times and will re-emerge as a national leader of efficient production and favourable living conditions.

The commune of Krynki could be considered as the opposite example to entrepreneurial Lomianki. This is a rural backward economic system, located by the border with Byelorussia. The population of 4100 inhabitants is getting smaller, due to constant outmigration. This population is dispersed in 29 locations, most of them not exceeding 40 inhabitants. Infrastructure is poor – there is no railway and telecommunication systems are outdated. Agriculture is by far the most dominant sector. However, it is poorly developed, farmers are getting old and the share of market production is low. There are only 79 private firms which give jobs to 157 persons, mostly operating in services oriented to the local (very small) market. The biggest firm employs ten people. Unemployment soars – there are 346 people without work. There are no institutions which would stimulate restructuring processes, run training and retraining courses, assist the private sector etc. No programme of local economic strategy exists. This commune would not be able to compete on the capital markets for new investment and for inflow of external (foreign or Polish) capital. To some extent, such an area is sentenced to stagnation and backwardness – at least in the foreseeable future.

Foreign Capital and a New International Setting

In Poland foreign firms were established as early as 1977 in six provinces of Poland, i.e. in Warsaw, Siedlce, Bielsko-Biala, Kraków, Czestochowa and Walbrzych voivodships. With time, more and more firms with foreign capital were installing themselves in large voivodship centres. This process was vastly accelerated after 1990.

It has been commonly accepted that the restructuring process cannot be performed without a massive inflow of foreign capital into the Polish economy. The first signs of this process can already be seen – by the end of 1993 some 3 billion US dollars were invested in Poland, and by mid-1995 the value of foreign investment in Poland reached 5.4 billion dollars (a further 5 billion were also committed). In the economic scenario it is envisaged that after the year 2000 the foreign capital inflow will reach 7–14 billion US dollars per annum.

The main regional concentrations of the involvement of foreign capital in Poland are presented in Table 3.8; Figure 3.14 presents the overall spatial differentiation of foreign investment in Poland.

Table 3.8 Foreign capital in Poland, 1993

No	Voivodships	Number of companies with foreign capital		
		In absolute numbers	Poland = 100	1991 = 100
1	Warsaw	3569	35.2	228
2	Gdansk	739	7.3	197
3	Poznan	705	7.0	184
4	Katowice	685	6.8	235
5	Szczecin	529	5.2	187
6	Wroclaw	452	4.5	228
7	Kraków	396	3.9	206
8	Lódz	371	3.7	183
9	Zielona Góra	224	2.2	215
10	Opole	185	1.8	240
	Poland	10,131	100.0	211

Source: Data from the Polish Agency for Foreign Investment

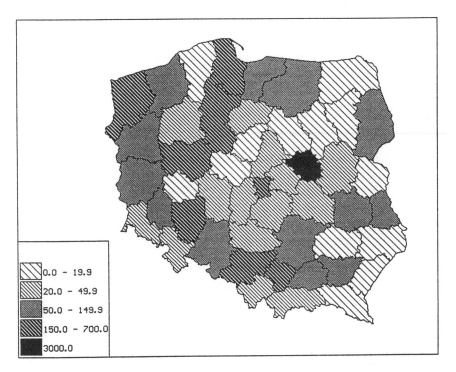

Source: Central Planning Office 1994

Figure 3.14 Foreign capital invested and declared to be invested in Poland, bln zl, March 1993

Among the first ten regions listed in the table we find two types of units: big cities, and regions located in the western part of the country. This pattern reflects the priorities of Western capital in locating its activities in Poland.

These first ten regions concentrate more than three-quarters of all joint ventures registered in Poland in 1992. They also present high dynamics of further growth. On the other side of the spectrum we find eastern voivodships, where there are very few such companies (Zamosc: 11; Ostroleka: 15; Lomza, Przemysl, Tarnobrzeg: all 16; Chelm, Krosno: both 17).

The regional distribution of foreign capital invested clearly indicates that – as in many other manifestations of transformation – also in this, the more advanced regions do find themselves in a more favourable situation. The pattern of the 'Letter L' is seen once again, plus the concentration of foreign investment in big cities. One may presume that the companies established in big cities are greater than those located in the peripheral regions.

Activities of foreign capital and international contacts of Polish businesses do not only change the economy. They also change the landscape of Polish cities. Warsaw, the biggest city and the greatest concentration of foreign investment, is perhaps the best example of these changes.

Changes are not only visible in the city centres. In peripheral concentrations of blocks with dwellings, which used to be infrastructural and commercial deserts, new initiatives emerge. Vietnamese restaurants appear, new newspaper stands with elegant designs flourish, services develop. On the previously sad and uninteresting route home from work, the inhabitants of such block compounds are increasingly confronted with advertisements, attractive windows of small shops, cafes and restaurants.

Over the last three to four years 33 new construction projects financed or co-financed by foreign capital have been finalised in Warsaw. These – usually – are office buildings and hotels of high standard. The following examples can be recalled:

- CURTIS PLAZA hosting offices, bank, hospital, shops, restaurant, parking for 300 cars, total floor area of $70,000m^2$, 6 floors;
- GREEN HOUSE (Elas Business), offices, $3600m^2$, 2 floors;
- FIM Tower – offices, exhibition halls, parking for 110 cars, $10,500m^2$, 25 floors, 3 buildings;
- IPC Business Centre – offices, bank, conference hall, shops, garage, $15,000m^2$;
- 'Silver Skyscraper' – offices, banks, exhibitions and conference halls, shops, restaurants, $27,000m^2$, 29 floors;Bank PeKaO SA – offices, $20,000m^2$, 22 floors;
- modernisation of the BRISTOL Hotel – 206 rooms, 43 apartments (the highest-standard hotel in Poland);

- Marriott Hotel, 521 rooms, 10 apartments.

A further 30 investments of this kind are planned in the near future. As a result, the city centre will soon change its outlook and its image – it will become a typical 'Western' modern city, with numerous offices, banks, restaurants, shops and diversified commercial profile. The sadness of the socialist city will soon disappear.

At least 15 foreign firms have invested more than 10 million US dollars in the Warsaw region. The biggest ones are the following: Curtis International, 100 million; PepsiCo, 78 million; International Finance Co., 68 million; Procter & Gamble, 60 million; Thomson, 60 million; Coca Cola, 56 million; RJ Reynolds, 50 million.

American capital invested in the region until the end of 1993 amounted to some 400 million US dollars, which is approximately 40 per cent of the total American investment in Poland and more than half of foreign capital invested in the Warsaw region. French (80 million US dollars) and German (75 million) investments come next.

These changes are not limited to the big cities. In a town of some 30,000 inhabitants the two competitive dealers of Peugeot and Renault share two opposite corners of the street. Ice-cream advertisements are displayed in small villages etc.

All these examples – from a sky-scraper and a luxurious hotel in a big city, through to an elegant shop in a medium-sized town and to a trademark sign in a village – are the manifestations of the new economic reality which change the landscape of the country, making it much more colourful and interesting, but also more frustrating for those who cannot benefit from this new reality.

These changes are also reflected in the price of land and its regional differentiation.

Prices per $1m^2$, thousands zl, end of 1992		
Town	Developed plots	Undeveloped plots
Bialystok	130–300	80 –130
Bytom	60–120	40–80
Kraków	30–400	10–80
Lublin	–	200
Lódz	150–160	15–50
Poznan	140–600	65–130
Torun	240–260	100–130
Warsaw	230–1400	50–130
Zielona Góra	300	–

Source Szul, Galazka and Mync (1993)

Polish regions have different standing as possible locations of investment. According to an already mentioned study,[6] Polish voivodships present deeply differentiated business attractiveness and climate for entrepreneurs. The following items were considered:

- the size of the regional market;
- the local labour market;
- the industrial background;
- the business environment;
- the quality of environment and tourist attractions;
- the industrial, telecommunication and transport infrastructure.

As could have easily been predicted, the most attractive regions are those which have a large agglomeration in their territory and the least attractive are the most backward central and eastern regions.

It is obvious that there is deep regional differentiation of foreign investment in Central Europe. Two types of regions are highly preferred by investors: big urban centres with good international (air) transport and telecommunication facilities, which – at the same time – may offer good living conditions, and the regions bordering Germany and Austria. International capital locates itself in the urban centres, the German capital concentrates in the western part of Poland and the Czech Republic. Relations between Austria and the western part of Hungary are rooted in tradition.

The eastern parts of the four countries, to a large extent, have been omitted by foreign capital. Hungary may be the sole exception to this rule, though much more was invested in Budapest and in the west than in the eastern part of this country.

The regional differentiation of the involvement of foreign capital in Central Europe is presented in Figure 3.15.

Spatial distribution of enterprises with participation by foreign capital in former *Czecho-Slovakia* (the data available refers to 1991–1992) fits neatly into a pattern. In Czecho-Slovakia one could notice a very distinct division between two federal republics. At the end of 1991 80 per cent of enterprises with a share of foreign capital were located within the Czech Republic. Similarly, the volume of capital was very unevenly distributed, namely 74.3 per cent of total capital was located in the Czech Republic, while only 25.7 per cent – in Slovakia. The data for 1992 indicated that these differences grew: 92.3 per cent of the total foreign capital invested in Czecho-Slovakia in that year was located in Bohemia, and only 7.7 per cent – in Slovakia. In Slovakia the greatest number of enterprises with foreign capital was concentrated in Bratislava, this being caused by the more difficult conditions encountered by foreign investors in this republic. Majority of German

---

6   'The map of investment risk', projected financed by Polski Bank Rozwoju, conducted by Instytut Badan nad Gospodarka Rynkowa, Warsaw-Gdansk, February 1994.

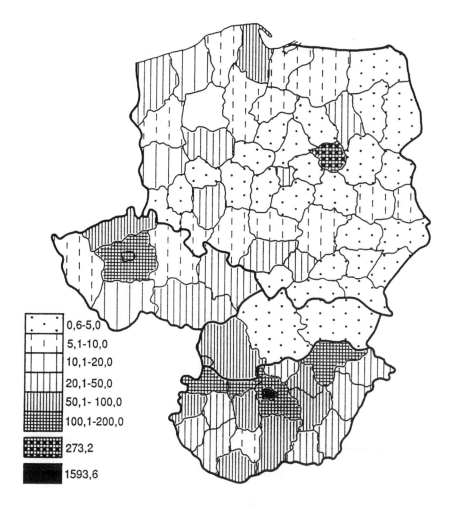

Figure 3.15 Foreign capital invested in regions of Central Europe, mln USD, 1992

Legend:
0,6-5,0
5,1-10,0
10,1-20,0
20,1-50,0
50,1- 100,0
100,1-200,0
273,2
1593,6

capital is concentrated in three regions: in central Bohemia (most of it), in Prague and in Bratislava. It is also interesting to note that at the beginning of 1992 German capital constituted 92.1 per cent of foreign capital invested in central Bohemia, 44.1 per cent in Prague and 66.1 per cent in Bratislava.

In *Hungary* the enterprises with foreign capital are present in all regions and the spatial distribution of these enterprises in Hungary is the most homogeneous of all four countries. The greatest number of enterprises with foreign capital and the greatest foreign capital value could be observed in Budapest and Pécs. Budapest concentrates the highest volume of foreign capital among all administrative units in Central Europe. Fejer and Borsod-Abúj-Zemplen also attract foreign investment.

The areas with the lowest rate of foreign investment were the Tolna, Heves, Nográd and Jász-Nagykun-Szolnok districts.

A comparison of Budapest, Prague and Warsaw with respect to the number of enterprises and the volume of foreign capital involved is presented in Table 3.9.

Table 3.9 Capitals of Central Europe as centres of location of foreign capital

Capitals	Number of firms with foreign capital in a given country = 100%	Total foreign capital in a given country = 100%
Budapest	31.12.1991 56.0%	31.12.1991 57.5%
Prague	5.10.1991 49.0%	31.12.1991 45.4% (without firms with 100% foreign share)
Warsaw	31.12.1991 32.6%	5.10.1991 39.4% (declared capital)

Source: Dziemianowicz 1993

As can be seen, among the capitals of the three states considered, it is Budapest that has the highest concentration of firms with foreign capital and the highest volume of capital itself. The relatively lower concentration of foreign investments in Warsaw is due to the existence, in Poland, of other large agglomerations, where investors locate their undertakings equally willingly. However, the role of Warsaw seems to be growing, since this city concentrates more and more of foreign capital invested in Poland (in March 1993 some 40% of capital and 35% of firms).

For all countries the inflow of foreign capital is regarded as one of the most important factors of transformation and development. This is true, even to a greater extent, of the regional economies. *It should not be expected that the already established locational patterns of foreign investment in Central Europe should change dramatically in the near future. The eastern backward regions will offer much less location advantages than the better developed core and capital cities. In this way foreign capital will become an additional factor in regional polarisation in Central Europe.*

The Central European economies used to have two important features: these were the economies mainly oriented towards the Eastern and Central European markets and these were the closed economies. Both these factors changed dramatically in 1989–1990. The impact of shifting the commercial contacts from East to West have already been covered. The role of opening the Central European countries to the world and the changes in their neighbours will play an important role for regional development, too.

The western and eastern borders of the three countries (Hungary, Poland, Slovakia) separate territorial systems of dramatically different levels of development and civilisational advancement. To a lesser extent this applies to the Czech Republic.

Eastern parts of Germany today are already far more developed than neighbouring Polish and Czech regions and this difference will grow as will a continued levelling out of the intra-German discrepancies.[7] The same applies to Austria, western regions of Hungary, southern regions of the Czech Republic and south-western Slovakia. In the same manner, Polish, Slovak and Hungarian eastern regions – even taking into account their relative underdevelopment – are much more advanced and better equipped with infrastructure than their neighbours in the East. Germany is perhaps still not less attractive for Polish workers than Poland for the incomers from the East. The crowds of small merchants coming from the former Soviet republics to Poland and selling their low-quality but cheap goods on the streets resemble the same floods of Polish people who sought their chances of extra income in Germany and other Western countries only four or five years ago. To some extent a more balanced situation exists between Hungary and Rumania and Slovenia.

In the case of Polish western regions all indicators demonstrate that only the agglomeration of Szczecin copes with the transformation processes relatively well. The city of Szczecin appears to be one of the leading centres of privatisation, involvement of foreign capital and industrial restructuring. It has relatively diversified economic structures and even its leading industry – shipbuilding – has proved able to survive the overall recession.

However, this positive influence of Szczecin is limited only to the city itself and adjacent areas. Even 50 to 70 kilometres eastward and southward the economic and social reality is dramatically different. The collapse of the state-owned agriculture became the most serious crisis factor and has led to massive unemployment. For example, in the Resko commune, located in the Szczecin voivodship 70 kilometres east of the city, the unemployment rate has reached 30 per cent.

The entire border belt south of Szczecin is in a similar situation to Resko. Unemployment rates are: 16.4 per cent in the Gorzów voivodship; 12.85 per cent in Zielona Góra; 16.8 per cent in Jelenia Góra. Only in the Szczecin voivodship is this rate smaller (10%).

The economic structures of these regions do not allow for rapid change in this situation. The natural increase in population numbers is higher than elsewhere in the country. In some regions (Jelenia Góra) the raw material extraction sectors (mainly brown coal), do not have any chance of survival in the long run and in the meantime pose great dangers for the already heavily polluted environment.

---

7   See Winiarski 1993. According to Winiarski, there are only few parts of the Polish–German border where the Polish potential may be comparable with the level of development of the German territories next to the common border.

High proportions of forest in Zielona Góra and Gorzów voivodships (the highest in Poland) predispose these areas to tourist services; however, the tourist infrastructure is poorly developed.

It may be predicted that the negative impact of isolation of the western border regions will be overcome via collaboration with more developed western neighbours. The geographical location alone of the 'western belt' may create its greatest potential. This is a region located centrally in Europe and is the closest to the Western centres of economic activity. It is also the natural 'border market' for Austrians and Germans, who take advantage of price differences and increase the demand for basic commodities and services. It is estimated, for example, that the German buyers leave some 4 billion DEM yearly in western Polish regions; similarly, for many years now the Austrians have taken advantage of cheaper goods and services in Hungary. There are also opportunities for the citizens of central Europe, who seek technically more advanced yet cheaper products in Germany (estimates indicate that a single Polish shopper 300–500 DEM).

Moreover, this is the region which has transport advantages for investors from Germany who seek cheaper labour and financial incentives for their production. The greatest agglomeration in Central Europe – Berlin – is just 70 kilometres from the Polish border and its positive (in economic terms) influence can already be seen in the form of investment and other commercial contacts. The same applies to Bratislava and to the western regions of Hungary and the Czech Republic. The Western border belts of Hungary, the Czech Republic and Poland have already attracted the attention of foreign (mostly German) investors and in several respects manifested their capabilities in the new economic system. Such a development of manufacturing and service sectors may give jobs to those currently unemployed. The proximity of the German market will, no doubt, be a positive factor.

Finally, mutual proximity encourages common programmes and projects, institution-building (like the international university in Frankfurt am Oder-Slubice, the Central European University in Prague and Budapest etc.). Some foundations for such benefits have already been laid in the so-called 'Stolpe Plan' which envisages the creation of the Euroregion of the Odra river. Another Euroregion, 'River Nysa', which encompasses the border areas of Germany, Poland and the Czech Republic, was created through German initiative in mid-1991. The Euroregion 'Pomerania' is still in the preparatory phase. Other Euroregions on the Polish–German border are also envisaged in the distant future.

Germany is much more involved and active in the creation of Euroregions with Polish towns and communes than Poland. Almost all initiatives and all investment already made is of German origin. Inequality of economic potential in several such projects is great, as, for example, in the projected 'Central Odra River' Euroregion on the latitude of Berlin. In several cases Polish and German economic interests may be mutually contradictory in such organisations. Agricultural production is the most sensitive topic – the Germans are afraid of the competition of cheaper Polish food products and try to secure decreases in Polish agricultural production in the border regions. In spite of these specific tensions, it is obvious that all parties may thus gain from multi-cultural contacts through a relatively open frontier.

However, further transfrontier cooperation in a situation of great inequality of economic potential may create both opportunities and dangers for the western border regions of Central Europe which are less developed than their neighbours. The problem of exploitation cannot be ruled out. This exploitation may assume the form of using the cheaper labour force for processing and manufacturing products sold under the German or Austrian name; of a massive inflow of German capital, which could lead to moving the decision-making centres outside of the country and even lead to political repercussions; of the process of deepening already existing inequality on the two sides of the common border; finally, the danger of incorporating Polish and Czech western border regions into the economic system of German – as the most distant periphery of this system – cannot be totally neglected. It is therefore the problem of policy, and not only of regional policy, to alleviate the dangers and to encourage the opportunities for Poland's western border regions. This will be discussed in the chapter presenting policy recommendations.

The border regions on the East are in a totally different position. The inequality between the areas located on the two sides of the frontier is in the opposite situation: Polish, Hungarian and Slovak territories, as backward as they are, are still better developed than the regions of the Ukraine, Byelorussia and Lithuania. However, the low level of development does not allow for too much optimism in predicting their future.

In general, the Eastern parts always used to be the most backward part of the three countries. Polish eastern territories always used to be the most backward part of the country. Only some central regions could be compared with these territories in terms of the low level of urbanisation, industrialisation and equipment with infrastructure. One may say, however, that the location factor – at least as it appears now – puts the Eastern territories in worse circumstances than the centre of the country.

The eastern part of Poland is predominantly agricultural in character. Only in the South did industry used to play a more important role; this was the effect of the industrialisation process undertaken within the Central Industrial District programme and then of further developments after World War Two. Agriculture is weak: underpopulated in the north, and overpopulated in the south. Agricultural culture is low, technological progress slow, equipment, machinery and capital poor.

Out of the three regional capitals of Eastern Poland, only Lublin has a long tradition of urbanisation and is fully equipped with cultural and educational institutions (two universities, several other academic institutions). Two other urban centres, Bialystok in the north and Rzeszów in the south have found historical opportunities only as replacements for the two other metropolises lost after the war to the former Soviet Union: Wilno (Vilnus, now the capital of Lithuania) and

Lwów (Lvov, now in the Ukraine). This accelerated development resulted in speedy advancement for these two towns. They were provided with university-level educational institutions (although the Medical Academy in Bialystok is the only one which ranks highly on the national scale) and have relatively high shares of professionals with university-level educational levels (for example in Rzeszów, 11 per cent of the population over 24 has attained this educational level, which is more than in Kraków).

One may say, however, that the location factor – at least as it appears now – puts the Eastern territories in a disadvantageous position when compared with other parts of these three countries.

Until now, the transformation *processes* had several negative sides for the entire Eastern *parts* of the *three countries (Hungary, Poland and Slovakia)*. Privatisation was slow and – in general – limited to trade. Involvement of foreign capital was minimal (see above). The rate of unemployment outside agriculture and in some parts of the region, and the average rate of unemployment, are higher than the national averages and job opportunities are few. The broken ties with the former Soviet market and the shrinking demand of the military are the most important causes of this especially deep recession. There is no immediate likelihood of commercial cooperation with the East reaching the scale once reached in the past. Eastern *parts of Hungary, Poland and Slovakia* must therefore seek other ways of revitalising *their economies.*

In particular, the southern part of Poland to a large extent followed the path of Starachowice. The prospects of the sulphur mining region are very bleak, due to the fall in sulphur prices and environmental problems that this activity creates. Central and northern parts of the Polish east were struck by the overproduction of food and by a deteriorating situation in the agricultural sector. Privatisation through liquidation was the most frequently used method, demonstrating the difficult economic situation of the privatised companies. Also the growth of the genuinely private sector (through private direct investment) was slower than elsewhere. Involvement of foreign capital was minimal. The rate of unemployment outside agriculture and in some parts of the region and the average rates of unemployment are higher than the national average and job opportunities are few. In some localities this rate reaches 30 per cent and in the North, in Suwaêki voivodships where, in addition to other manifestations of recession the state farms collapsed (this was the only part of the eastern belt where the state sector had a high share in agriculture), this rate reached 40–50 per cent.

The eastern belt must therefore seek other ways of revitalising its economy. The proximity of the border could be considered as one of the development factors. However, until now this influence is relatively weak and consists, mostly, of the development of the 'grey' economy. Poland and Hungary are attractive markets for the small businessmen from the former Soviet republics. These countries also offer better employment opportunities and living standards than the homeland.

To some extent this inflow of cheap goods may jeopardise local manufacturing and local labour markets.

However, this may have some positive multiplier effects on the economy of the eastern border regions of the three countries. Local consumers save on their basic spending. Several small businesses make their living on this illegal or semi-legal trade. Some services emerge oriented towards the visitors from the East. Primary accumulation of capital may be the result of these operations, which may be important for these relatively poor regions.

In any case, it has to be openly stated that Hungarian, Polish and Slovak eastern border regions do have much reduced opportunities for economic and cultural advancement than the Western border belt. Both the starting position and the character of their neighbours put the East on more difficult terrain. Over the next 10 to 15 years (and presumably even longer) the Central European Eastern belt will still be the least developed part of the three countries, no matter what kind of regional or other policies are formulated and implemented.

The same applies also to the eastern regions of the Czech Republic, for which their Slovak neighbours do not create many opportunities for benefits stemming from trans-border cooperation. A similar pattern may also be found in the south-eastern regions of Hungary, neighbouring Rumania.

Mutual cooperation of the Polish, Czech, Slovak and Hungarian regions is an open question. More problems have emerged since 1989 than have been solved. The chance of the most promising cases for cooperation, like the Polish–Czech town of Cieszyn divided by the national border, have been utilised on a much lower level than has happened in another similar town, Slubice/Frankfurt am Oder, divided by the Polish–German border. The Gabcikovo–Nagymaros case (the dam on the Danube, which is strongly favoured by the Slovaks and strongly opposed by the Hungarians) should not become the model of trans-border relations for the Central European border regions.

Such contacts may also have other positive effects. The cultural dimension of exchange of people, ideas and information is of even greater importance than on the western borders of Central Europe. Meeting other people creates personal ties which may be stronger than traditional stereotypes. There has been a lot of hostility between Poles and Ukrainians and even between Poles and Lithuanians (although in this last case contemporary politicians may have had their negative influence). These hostilities have had little opportunity to be eliminated, since the 'frontiers of friendships' between the former socialist countries (especially those with the former Soviet Union) were sealed ones. For example, it should not be hidden that on both sides of the Polish–Ukrainian border some mutual tensions still exist. To a great extent they are rooted in history. However, some recent deeds of Polish politicians also have their negative impact. Some of them tend to bring into former Soviet republics the 'civilisation mission' which does not – naturally – meet with friendly attitudes there. Extending influence of the catholic church into predomi-nantly orthodox areas – under the banner of providing a Polish minority with religious assistance – has been met with a very negative reception. In some respects these phenomena may explain the inefficiency of Polish attempts to speed up transborder cooperation in science and culture.

All such activities to some extent *might* resemble some manifestations of German feelings of superiority towards Polish western border regions. In both cases – although tensions in the West seem to be less significant than in the East – this may hamper trans-border cooperation and reduce the advantages of multi-cultural exchange in economic, cultural and scientific fields.

In spite of these difficulties, new contacts may allow better mutual learning of national and regional cultures, thus introducing the spirit of cooperation and true friendship. These stereotypes break down in confrontation with real life. This creates grounds for future economic and cultural cooperation with neighbours on both sides of the border.

The most recent initiative of the Euroregion Karpatia may be considered as a good example of new developments in international relations of the Polish south-eastern regions with their neighbours. On February 14 1993 the foreign ministers of Hungary, Poland, Slovakia and Ukraine signed an agreement constituting this Euroregion. It is composed of three Hungarian regions, two Polish, six Slovak districts and one Ukranian province. The Euroregion will promote mutual international contacts between the member regions, their authorities and citizens and between enterprises located on their territories.

It has to be admitted that the idea of Euroregion Karpatia was challenged by some political forces in Poland. It was indicated that as well as positive results it could bring several negative, such as organised crime, an uncontrolled inflow of people, smuggled goods etc. Some of these arguments were obviously following the general, almost chavinist, ideologies of these parties – however, these arguments cannot be easily dismissed on purely rational grounds. These reservations illustrate the possible negative side-effects of transborder contacts on the Eastern Polish frontier.

Regional Structure of Economic Power

For several years now the list of the 500 biggest enterprises in Poland has been compiled, published and analysed. The regional structure of basic indicators derived from this list creates excellent grounds for examining the regional structure of economic power.

The firms listed there are – in many cases – multi-branch companies which have their subsidiaries in several locations all over the country. They are listed in the region in which their headquarters is located. Therefore, the regional distribution of particular indicators provides information on the regional structure of economic control of the biggest companies in Poland.

The first companies on the list are the following: the oil refinery in Plock (approximately 2 billion US dollars of sales), Ciech (foreign trade agency for chemical products), Bank Handlowy (commercial bank), Bank PKO – all three in Warsaw, Weglokoks in Katowice, (foreign trade company dealing in coal), Gdansk Refinery, KGHM Polska Miedz in Lubin (copper mining and processing), Agricultural Bank in Warsaw and FSO car factory in Warsaw. These are the state-owned companies which also existed before and have not been restructured as yet. The first private firm on the list (Elektrim – operating in trade) occupies 13th position. Only a few entries on the list represent newly established firms with private capital. However, some of the companies have been sold to foreign owners or are partly owned by foreign capital. The last firms on the list have had sales of some 3–4 million US dollars.

Companies on the list employ almost 1 million persons, out of which 30 per cent are employed by firms located in Warsaw. The share of Warsaw is the greatest in banking: out of 48 banks present on the list 20 are located in Warsaw itself and Warsaw concentrates two-thirds of total employment and total turnover of all Polish banks.

Figures 3.16 and 3.17 present the number of companies and employment of the 500 biggest Polish firms, respectively. Once again, as in several other indicators, the 'letter L' pattern is clearly visible in the figures. Two regions clearly break out of this pattern, with the greatest concentration of big firms: the Warsaw and Katowice regions. However, these two regions also lead in other spheres, which have been examined so far. The role of these two voivodships in hosting headquarters of big companies is obvious: Warsaw is the location of several national public companies, such as Post and Telecommunication, Polish Railways, and also of several banks, both privatised and public. The Katowice voivodship is the location of the seven holdings which group coal mines, big steel mills and chemical plants and foreign trade companies dealing in coal.

The following voivodships host the greatest numbers of big companies: Warsaw, 83; Katowice, 70; Gdansk, 26; Poznan, 25; Kraków and Lublin, 20 each; Bydgoszcz and Szczecin, 19 each; Kalisz and Kielce, 17 each; Wroclaw, 16; Lódz, 15.

Eastern and western parts of Poland host very few big firms. *In four voivodships (Chelm, Ciechanów, Sieradz, Slupsk) no firm from the list of the biggest 500 existed in 1992. In several others there are just one or two such companies.*

Even greater discrepancies exist in terms of the sales figures of the big firms. Companies which have their headquarters in big cities are usually bigger – have greater sales and employ more people.

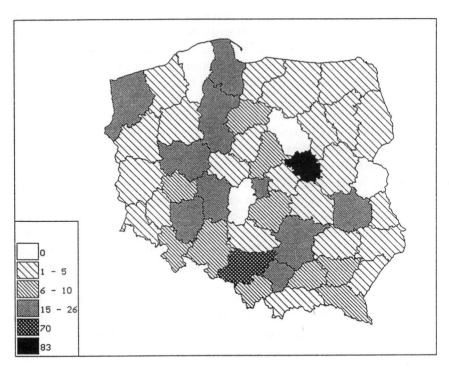

Figure 3.16 Number of firms from the list of 500 biggest Polish companies, 1992

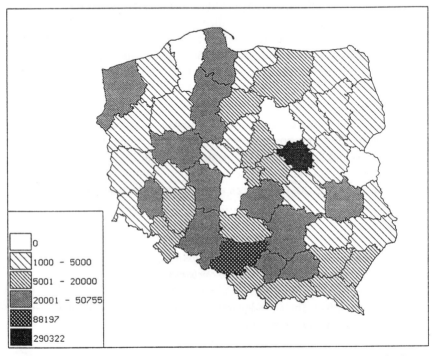

Figure 3.17 Number of employees in the firms from the list of 500 biggest companies in Poland, 1992

The list is rather stable over time. Comparison with the arrangement of the biggest enterprises in Poland for 1991 does not show too many changes of positions. Only few companies changed their position by more than 100 places and even less got into the list in 1992 (the biggest advance was made by the private firm Elektromis operating in commerce, which in 1992 was in 89th place and in the previous year was absent from the list). This is rather strange in times of rapid structural changes and leads to the conclusion that the situation of the biggest companies is more stable than that of smaller firms.

The list of 500 biggest companies in Poland is a product of the past economic reality. New entries of private firms, with capital of both Polish and foreign origin, will demonstrate the pace of the systemic transformation of the Polish economy.

The first manifestations of these processes are already covered by statistical data. The list of the 100 biggest private firms in Poland has been recently published for 1992.[8] Several firms present on this list had been state-owned and then privatised. However, the first two firms: Elektrim and Profus Management are of genuine private origin.

Transport Links with Europe[9]

Transport connections establish the 'spatial skeleton' of a given economic system. Transport infrastructure lines create a web, constructed on the main nodes – the urban centres which concentrate economic, political and cultural activities. These nodes and the areas adjacent to the main connecting lines have the greatest opportunity for constant and fast development.

Poland has relatively well developed rail connections. There are 23,000 kms of railways, out of which 8000 kms carry transit in an east–west direction. However, even the rails need modernisation and improvement of speed and safety standards. The same applies to loading/unloading facilities of the main rail stations. International transport by Polish firms has only a 7 per cent share of all cargo transported in Poland. This share may grow up to 10 per cent in the near future.

There are 232,000 kms of roads in Poland, and 46,000 kms are prepared for accommodation of international transit. These roads are, however, relatively poor quality – there are only a few sections of modern highways, not more than 300 kms in the entire country. The modernisation of the road network is one of the most important tasks of Polish transformation.

Since 1980 there has been a constant decline of international cargo transport. In 1992 the weight of goods transported by Polish carriers into Poland from abroad constituted only some 30 per cent of the 1980 level, goods transported

8   'Wprost', no 49, 5 December 1993.
9   This section is based on the material prepared by the Central Planning Office 1993 *The Concept of Development of International and Domestic Transport Connections.*

out of Poland 80 per cent and goods carried through Poland 30 per cent. All shipments of goods (inflow, outflow, transit) carried out by Polish carriers decreased from 142 million tons in 1980 to 73 million tons in 1992. This decrease was partly compensated by foreign carriers (it is impossible to estimate to what extent due to lack of data). During the last two years this decrease has been halted and by 1995 stabilisation of shipment by Polish firms is envisaged. After 1995 some growth may happen, up to 150 per cent of the 1992 level in the year 2000.

The share of road transport will constantly increase, at the expense of rail shipments. Already in 1992 the number of trucks crossing the Polish border grew by 50 per cent in comparison with 1991 and further fast growth is inevitable.

Passenger transport by public services (rail, bus, air, sea) has decreased, too, though not at the same pace as transport of commodities. There were 10.3 million such international journeys in 1992, as compared with 13.6 million in 1990. This decrease was more than compensated by international journeys by passenger cars. In 1991 the Polish borders were crossed by 114 million people and in 1992 by 194 million. In 1992 49 million foreigners visited Poland and 30 million Polish citizens left the country. This movement is very likely to grow in the future, with Poland's increasing openness, the growth of incomes and the lifting restrictions in international travel.

The border crossing is one of the most severe barriers in further development of international contacts, in both commodity and passenger transport. At present, there are 118 road border crossings in Poland, but only 30 of them are used by more than 1 million persons and 9 by more than 5 million persons per annum. These are the following:

- on the eastern border: Terespol and Medyka;
- on the southern border: Cieszyn, Kudowa and Zgorzelec;
- on the western border: Slubice-Swiecko, Olszyna, Kolbaskowo.

Among the rail border crossings only the crossings at Kunowice and Zebrzydowice (on the southern Polish border) were used by more than 3 million passengers and a further five by more than 1 million. Medyka and Terespol/Malaszewice are by far the crossings shipping most cargo, around 9000 million tons each per annum.

The international airport in Warsaw should be added to this list with its 1.8 million passengers crossing the Polish border there, of which half were foreigners. No other Polish airport may compete with Warsaw in this respect – Kraków with 70,000 passengers (out of which 46,000 foreigners) and Gdansk (50,000 total traffic, 28,000 foreigners) are the next airports for international traffic. All other Polish airports do not have traffic greater than 17,000 passengers yearly altogether.

It is envisaged that international passenger travel will grow at a rapid pace in the near future, up to 300–350 million border crossings in the year 2000 and then stabilise. The number of crossings will grow up to 260, out of which 61 will be on the eastern border, 131 on the southern and 39 on the western. Road border crossings will be the most numerous (174).

The border crossings are only one part of the entire system of international flows of people and goods entering, leaving or crossing the country. These flows concentrate within the corridors, in which roads, railways and waterways are located.

Figure 3.18 presents transport corridors in Poland as envisaged after the year 2000 and Figure 3.19 presents a more detailed picture of main road connections. The transport connections displayed on these figures are incorporated into wider programmes of trans-European rail and road networks. Three corridors will play the most important role: two in an east–west direction (one central and one southern), and one (central) on the north–south axis. All these corridors will be filled by highways and railroads meeting the requirements of fast trains (the first fast train will be in operation on the Berlin–Moscow route, which will run parallel to the east–west central highway). By 1997, 350 kms of highways are to be constructed and the entire programme is to be finished by 2007.

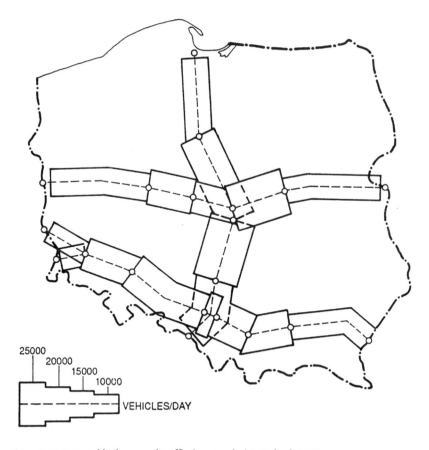

Figure 3.18 Expected highways and traffic (cars per day) in Poland, 2000

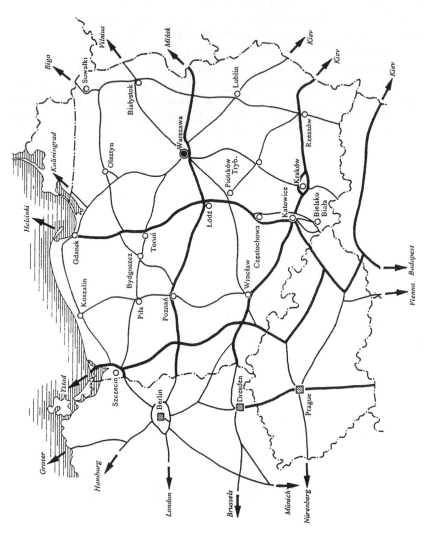

Figure 3.19 Major road connections of Poland, around the year 2000

These plans are in congruence with the projected dynamics of the movement of people and goods in the two strategic directions: east–west and north–south. According to the estimates of the Ministry of Transport, the east–west direction is – currently – more promising than the north–south one. Poland seems to have already lost the competition with former East Germany in capturing the north–south transport. This direction, in the light of instability in the Balkans and prospected accession of the Nordic countries to the European Union, has now become of secondary importance. The east–west direction became, therefore, even more important and of a greater strategic importance for a country with such a particular location as Poland. It is estimated that even during the next two years the overall transit transport in the westerly direction should increase by 60 per cent, while on the north–south axis traffic should only increase by 30 per cent. In any case, Poland will be in open competition with the three other Central European countries which also claim to be strategically located and which are also trying to capture as much of the east–west transit as possible.

Mutual economic relations between the four Central European countries have decreased considerably. In 1992 Czecho-Slovakia participated in 4–5 per cent and Hungary in less than 1 per cent of Polish foreign trade. Poland's exports to Czecho-Slovakia declined by less than 20 per cent, and to Hungary by about 33 per cent. Moreover, the structure of Polish exports to the other three Central European countries deteriorated, leaning towards the growth in the share of unprocessed products (raw materials), at the expense of machinery and manufactured goods. All four countries turned to the West and the importance of the Eastern markets declined sharply. It may be expected that this is a temporary decline and that mutual co-operation will redevelop on new principles and with a different structure. On the other hand, possible future development of trade between the West and the reformed former Soviet republics makes the Visegrad group an important transitory territory connecting East to West. In this light, the east–west transportation connections seem to gain in importance, which will call for an accelerated development of a modern transport infrastructure, especially of roads and fast railway connections.

The prospected changes in the transportation networks will be subordinated to two main principles: incorporation of Central Europe into a wider European network and improvement of quality. Highways and fast trains are the most important developments, already planned in all four countries. Construction of highways from Nurenberg to Prague and extending the German motorway from Berlin to Warsaw is of the highest priority. Moreover, in Hungary the pattern of subordination of the transportation network to Budapest is considered as the main task of developing a national transport infrastructure.

The international airports in Prague, Budapest and Warsaw should be considered as the most important gateways to Central Europe and transit points further to the east. Their current standard seems to be sufficient to meet demand during the next ten years, though a construction of a new passenger and cargo airport north of Warsaw should be undertaken. No other airports may compete with these three (Bratislava will retain its national character).

Natural Environment[10]

It has been commonly assumed that Poland, along with other socialist countries, has been one of the most polluted countries in Europe. The mistaken strategies of socialist industrialisation neglected the environmental dimension of development for a considerably longer period of time than was the case in the Western world. To a great extent this bleak picture should now be revised.

In Poland, 27 'hot spots' were officially recognised in 1983 and – as 'areas of ecological hazard' – given special status in some policy decisions. Of the 27, two areas come on the top of the list: the Legnica-Glogów Copper Basin, and the Katowice-Rybnik Coal Basin. This is geographically linked to the Czech Ostrava region.

Without doubt the worst situation has existed and still exists in Upper Silesia. Its economy emits into the environment 742 dangerous pollutants. This region 'produces' 25 per cent of all industrial dusts, 28 per cent of all gases, 25 per cent of all non-cleaned sewage and 57 per cent of all industrial solid waste. Ecological norms are exceeded by up to 12 times. However, there are localities in the region where these norms are being exceeded by 100–200 times. On 72 per cent of the region's territory noise exceeds the norms. All these environmental hazards have direct influence on the state of health of inhabitants of the region. There are 10 per cent more deaths resultant from cancer than the national average, 20 per cent more due to heart diseases. Of all women 45 per cent have their pregnancies in jeopardy and 10 per cent of births are premature.

There are other regions in Poland where the natural environment is dramatically endangered. Copper mining basin near Legnica is the most obvious example of an industrial region on the edge of an environmental catsatrophe. Forests in the south western corner of Poland (also polluted by Czech and East German industries) have died almost entirely. In fact, each of Poland's industrial centres creates danger to the environment. Some 12 million people live in unhealthy conditions; 27 areas have been labelled as endangered by pollution (see Figure 3.20).

On the other hand, Poland still possesses several large areas almost completely clean and unspoiled by unwise human activity. According to some estimates[11] 8.5 per cent of Polish territory remains relatively untouched by the negative sides of economic development. Forests and farms operating with sustainable and ecologically acceptable principles make up about 19 per cent of Polish territory. Hence, over a fourth of Poland represents an asset that many areas of Europe no longer

---

10　The study by Zylicz and Lehoczki (1994) has been extensively used in this section.
11　Zylicz and Spyrka (1993) several theses of this study have been recalled in this section.

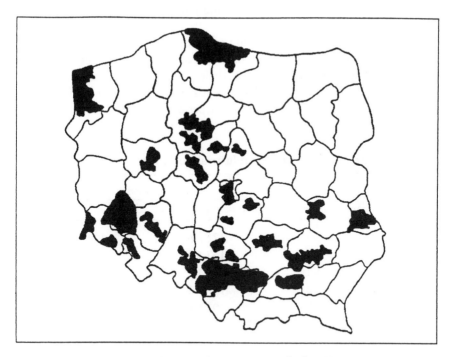

Figure 3.20 Twenty-seven areas of endangered environment in Poland, 1980s

have. These clean Polish areas maintain an ecological balance on much wider geographical scale and create a reservoir of really natural environment.

Poland's biological diversity is high, particularly with respect to forest and bog communities. In the last 400 years, the Polish vertebrate fauna has lost 15 species (2.5%), including 3 mammals, 11 birds and 1 fish species. At the same time, the Polish flora has lost 31 species of vascular plants. Sad as they are, these figures, however, turn out to be much less alarming than in other, more developed, European countries in the same biogeographical zone.

The ecological value of Poland's natural capital has been internationally recognised. All of its 17 national parks are on the IUCN list, as they meet all the criteria for this high degree of protection. Three of them have been included by UNESCO in a network of biosphere reserves representing typical well-preserved examples of the world's ecosystems. One of them – the Bialowieza National Park (whose natural extension in Byelorussia has also enjoyed the status of a national park) has been declared an object of exceptional importance to World Heritage, as the last remaining area of characteristic Central European lowland primeval forest.[12] Also a number of smaller areas, 'nature reserves', were found to be of

---

12 See, for example, report by Maddox 1994.

international importance, some of them being protected under the Ramsar Convention on wetland ecosystems.

The environment seems to be gaining considerably from the overall recession and the decrease of production, not only in Poland but also in neighbouring countries which traditionally 'exported' their pollution to Poland (mainly the former GDR and the Czech Republic). Recent statistics prove that both emission and imission of pollution decreased during the period 1989–1992 (see Table 3.10) and this process has been maintained in the years since then.

Table 3.10 Emission of industrial pollution in Poland

Years	Sewage in hms^3	Air pollution	
		Dusts in thousand tons	Gases in thousand tons
1985	11,115.1	1787.8	4932.5
1988	10,082.4	1614.5	5193.2
1989	10,314.1	1513.3	5112.6
1990	9486.4	1163.0	4114.6
1991	8792.7	923.1	3552.1

Source: Berger 1992, p. 166

To some extent this was also the result of growing efforts to stop the further increase of pollution in Poland. Public and private outlays directed at environmental protection have grown over the years: from 540 million US dollars in 1988 to 850 million in 1992 (in 1991 US dollars). These sums represent between 0.6 and 1.1 per cent of GDP in respective years. In terms of the structure of this expenditure, water protection and utilisation of solid waste lost to air protection, which consumed almost half of all means spent on the environment. Of these funds 40 per cent has been collected as pollution charges from the pollutants (already these charges are relatively high by OECD standards).

The whole of Central Europe no doubt used to be 'the basin of dirt' of the entire continent. Only the southern part of the former GDR and some coal mining and heavy industry centres in the former Soviet Union might have entered into this negative competition with the four Central European countries, although recent restructuring has led to substantial improvement in some regions.

Emissions of many pollutants – in particular, sulphur dioxide, untreated sewage, etc. – reached their peak levels in the 1980s, and are declining now. Still, in 1992 if compared with GDP, these emissions are remarkably higher than in Western Europe (see Table 3.11). Furthermore, the 'environmental performance' gap between East and West has increased during the last couple of years. This was a combined effect of two trends: the slower decline of pollution levels and the negative GDP growth rates in Central Europe (this has alredy begun to change, after turning into positive rates of growth).

Table 3.11 Pollution levels in Central Europe in 1991

kg/1000$	Dust (per unit of GDP) kg/1000$	SO^2 (per unit of GDP) m^3/1000$	Untreated sewage (per unit of GDP)
The Czech Republic[a]	30	50	–
Hungary	4	29	13
Poland	11	24	14
Slovakia[a]	21	41	55
The European Community	0.8	3	0.8[b]

Notes: [a]Gross Material Product (which is typically lower than GDP)
[b]Only the Federal Republic of Germany, 1987.
Source: Zylicz and Spyrka 1993.

Much of the East–West difference in this respect can be explained in terms of excessive energy use characteristic of the centrally planned economies of Central Europe. This is, however, only part of the story, and the environmental failure of communist regimes in Europe has to be seen in a much broader perspective.

The impact of the relatively high aggregate pollution levels is further amplified by their highly uneven spatial distribution. As a result, a number of areas throughout Central Europe have been suffering from particularly high doses of pollution (see Figure 3.21).

Two areas in the Czech Republic – besides the Czech part of Upper Silesia – are identified as heavily affected. These are: north Bohemia – where many power plants are concentrated – and Prague. The high level of industrial development combined with the reliance on coal deposits of poor quality are responsible for extremely high energy consumption and CO_2 emissions (4 tonnes per inhabitant per year – the highest in Europe). A number of pollutants emitted in the process of burning fossil fuels pose a direct threat to the environment and public health. Additionally, the country is affected by its nuclear industry. Chemicals used in processing the locally extracted uranium ore represent a serious risk for ground water contamination. The Temelín nuclear power plant has been the object of concern for its unproved safety system.

The extent of environmental disruption in Slovakia is rather low if measured by Polish or Czech standards. Sixteen areas – scattered around the country – are listed as those suffering from adverse environmental impacts. One has to observe, however, that this category includes also relatively unpolluted areas, like the Poprad Valley adjacent to the southern slope of the Tatra Mountains, which is simply affected by tourism. There are two areas which have been identified as

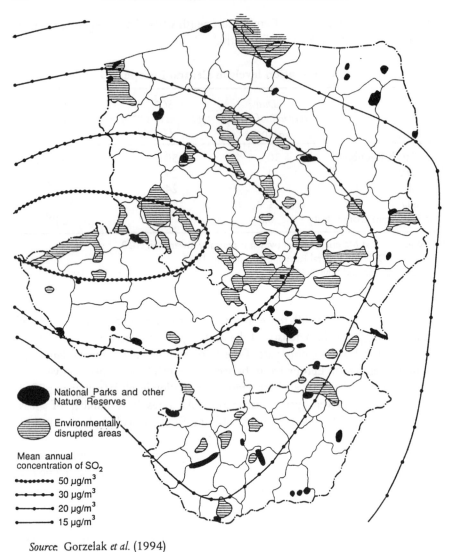

National Parks and other
Nature Reserves

Environmentally
disrupted areas

Mean annual
concentration of SO$_2$

●●●●●●● 50 µg/m^3
●━●━●━● 30 µg/m^3
●━━━● 20 µg/m^3
●━━━━ 15 µg/m^3

Source: Gorzelak *et al.* (1994)

Figure 3.21 Natural environment of Central Europe

heavily disrupted. One is the Upper Nitra River Valley where the disruption is caused by coal mining activities coupled with the development of heavy industries (chemicals, building materials and power generation). The other one is the East Slovak Range affected by the emissions from the local power plants, as well as chemical, timber and paper and pulp industries. In addition, both the major cities – Bratislava and Kosice – are considered serious problem areas too.

In Hungary most of the hot spots are located along the 'industrial axis' of the country that goes from south west to north east and includes Pécs in the south. It also includes several 'new socialist' towns, such as Ajka, Inota, Varpalota, Dorog, Dunaujváros, Lábatlan, Ozd and Százhalombatta, and big cities such as Budapest and Miskolc. In 1990, 12 cities from this region declared themselves as the dirtiest ones in the country. They are aiming at developing a programme to improve their disastrous environmental quality. Unfortunately, such initiatives have proved to be rather ineffective due to the economic recession which is very deep in these regions. The other hot spot areas are linked to the high level of hydrocarbon and lead concentrations along busy roads, particularly in Budapest.

There is no question about the generally declining pollution levels since the late 1980s. In Poland, they decreased by more than 30 per cent between 1988 and 1992. Likewise, in Slovakia particulate matter emissions decreased by 43 per cent, SO_2 emissions by 38 per cent. Some other pollutants (e.g. carbon monoxide) started to decline after 1989, yet other (e.g. nitrogen oxides and hydrocarbons) – after 1990. In the Czech Republic, a moderate decline in particulate matter emissions has continued since 1980 but the process was intensified after 1989. Between 1989 and 1991 emissions of particulates decreased by 12 per cent, SO_2 by 11 per cent, and nitrogen oxides by 20 per cent. In Hungary, the emission of particulate matter declined by 42 per cent, SO_2 by 34 per cent and NO_x by 17 per cent between 1988 and 1991.

It should be observed that as a rule, these rates are higher than the decline in GDP, and thus cannot be seen merely as a consequence of lower production. Consequently, *this downward-sloping trend is likely to be sustained at the same time as the economic recovery now under way.* Of course, the question about the pace of this process remains an unanswered one.

The most striking feature of the last period is *the increase in the share of expenditures aimed at air protection.* This share almost quadrupled in Slovakia between 1988 and 1991, doubled in Poland, and more than doubled in Hungary between 1988 and 1992. Three factors may influence this pattern. First, water protection programmes – as those which typically do not require a very high level of technological sophistication – have been implemented since long ago and as a result, towards the end of the 1980s, water quality could be considered as better than the air quality. Second, transboundary air-borne pollutants attracted much more international attention than the water-borne ones. Third, CE governments might have recognised that public health is at greater risk from air pollution exposure than from water pollution.

A declining trend in the Hungarian environmental investment until 1991 was the combined effect of inflation and of an approximately constant nominal level of expenditures. The latter can be interpreted as resulting from the lack of any new regulation to stimulate more efforts at abatement.

Although the environmental problems in Central Europe are enormous, they are not irreparable and hopeless. Further, *certain regions of Central Europe still enjoy a high degree of ecological soundness and biodiversity.*

Polish ecological assets have already been described above. All three of the *Czech* national parks are, in fact, international ones, as their management is co-ordinated with the corresponding units across the country's boundary: Karkonosze with Poland, Sumava with Germany, and Podyji with Austria. Two of the 27 landscape parks – Trebonsko and Krivoklátsko – have been included in the UNESCO network of biosphere reserves. At least ten others can be considered as areas of international importance because of their flora and geology.

Slovakia is particularly abundant with areas of unique ecological value enjoying the status of protected sites. Its five national parks cover almost 5 per cent of the country's area. In addition, 16 protected landscape zones were established in 13 per cent of the total area. These two categories together with their buffer zones comprise as much as 27 per cent of Slovak territory. There is also a large number of smaller sites under protection. More than 90 per cent of protected areas represent mountain ecosystems. Five sites are registered under the Ramsar Convention. Several others are planned to be included in the World Heritage list.

Hungary also has a number of ecologically valuable areas of international importance. As many as 13 sites are protected under the Ramsar Convention. There are also five areas listed as biospheric reserves. One of these, Fertö Lake, is planned to become an international park (with Austria).

Quite paradoxically, the natural capital which survived several decades of the communist mismanagement is now under serious threat from a new sort of development. Even though the logic of market economies is likely to lead to more efficient resource use, at the same time, it exposes these resources to new pressures resulting from their opening up to large-scale international tourism and international real estate markets. The Sumava National Park is reported to be experiencing the tourism pressure which increased rapidly after the collapse of the previous political system. Similar problems are observed in many areas of western and northern Poland, which mostly attract German tourists.

Immense as they are, environmental problems in Central Europe are neither unique nor irreparable. The awareness of this fact is not universal, but the Central European countries have an opportunity for recovery from the current predicament which very much resembles that of Western Europe and the United States in the 1960s. *It is not unrealistic to expect that they will be able to eliminate most of the severe environmental risks to human health by the end of the decade. At the same time, it is unlikely that they will succeed in decontaminating all the hot spots, as some of them – sealed off from the public – will have to wait for immediate risks to be addressed first and for recultivation technologies to become realistically available.*

To a large extent, Central Europe can replicate the OECD experience, where the recovery was accomplished after two decades of steady investment in abatement equipment and structural adjustments following environmental regulation and growing energy prices. This process, however, can either be accelerated by well-conceived integrated economic and environmental policies or delayed if economic reforms drag and environmental requirements are perceived as constraints on the continued growth of old industries. *Thus the success of the environmental recovery process crucially depends on the success of economic reforms.*

The Political Profiles of Polish Regions

It is very difficult to report on the regional political profiles in a situation, where the national political stage is still in a process of being furnished and the national political structures are still being created. However, some very general tendencies are visible on the political map of Poland.

Since 1989 there have been several elections conducted in a democratic way. The parliamentary elections of June 1989 ended communist rule in the country. This political event, to a great extent, was similar to the local elections one year later (May 1990). In both cases a kind of 'zero-one' solution was adopted: the representatives of the old regime were confronted with the unified new political power affiliated to the post-Solidarity circles – at that time, union leader, Lech Walesa. The presidential elections (November–December 1990) and two consecutive parliamentary elections (November 1991 and September 1993) were conducted in a more complex, 'multi-choice' political setting.

Statistical analyses of the regional results of these few political events – the turn-out and the political preferences of the electorate – reveal two major spatial dimensions of electoral behaviour in Poland (as we remember from pp.00–00, these general dimensions also structure other features of Polish socio-economic space):

1. urban–rural differences;

2. historical profiles of regions.

Urban–rural differences manifest themselves in the support given to particular parties. Several parties (Democratic Union, Liberal-Democratic Congress,[13] and Union of Real Policy) appeared to gain followers only in towns, and especially in big cities, while other parties found their electorate in the rural areas (Polish Peasant Party, Peasant Agreement).

These divisions reveal the class character of the political system in Poland. The 'urban' parties are the parties of the educated social strata, the white-collar workers, who are concentrated in big urban centres. The support for the blue-collar workers' parties is split between the parties of post-communist origin and the post-Solidar-

---

13 In April 1994 these two parties merged and created the Union of Liberty (Unia Wolnosci).

ity ones and is not connected to any type of locality. The parties appealing to the rural electorate, especially the Polish Peasant Party, want to become national and classless, but – until now – these attempts have not been successful.

The historical patterns of political behaviour manifest themselves in the division of the country into territories of the 19th century partitions of Poland between Prussia, Russia and Austria. The most clearly pronounced spatial difference in political behaviour is the difference between the four parts of the country:

- the former Russian part (central and eastern Poland),

- the Austrian part (Galicia).

The first one being much more left-oriented than the second (see Figures 3.22 and 3.23).

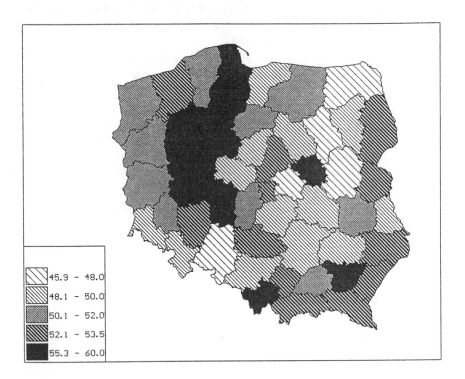

45.9 – 48.0
48.1 – 50.0
50.1 – 52.0
52.1 – 53.5
55.3 – 60.0

Source: Zarycki (1994)

Figure 3.22 Turn-out, parliamentary elections in poland, September 1993

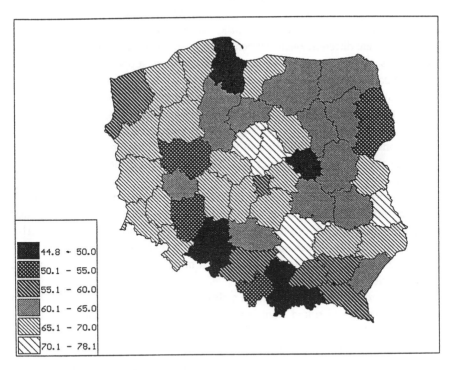

44.8 – 50.0
50.1 – 55.0
55.1 – 60.0
60.1 – 65.0
65.1 – 70.0
70.1 – 78.1

Source: Zarycki (1994)

Figure 3.23 Votes against the course of economic reforms, parliamentary elections in Poland, September 1993

The detailed study[14] of the political behaviour of the Tarnobrzeg voivodship (south eastern part of the country) fully confirms these national observations on the local scale. The region is divided into two historical parts: the former Austrian and Russian parts. In all elections after 1989 in the Austrian part of the voivodship the turnout was higher and the support for the post-Solidarity parties higher than in the former Russian part. These differences only to some extent can be explained by the differences in the historical and contemporary economic and social structures, and the traditions of political consciousness do play an important role.

14 Zarycki 1994.

It is possible to have another interpretation of the political profiles at regional level. The 'core', highly urbanised regions (i.e. those with big urban centres: Warsaw, Lódz, Poznan, Wroclaw, Kraków, Gdansk, Szczecin, Katowice and Bielsko-Biala) do demonstrate different electoral behaviour from the eastern part of the country. The voters in the core areas expressed much higher support for the previous, post-Solidarity government of the Prime Minister H. Suchocka and – in fact – rejected the two leftist parties which won the last election. In the above-mentioned regions the PSL–SLD coalition (peasant and social democrats) received only 69 seats in the parliament, while all other parties received 82 seats. In the regions which constitute the former Russian part of Poland these proportions were the opposite: the two winning parties won 100 seats in parliament while the other parties won only 17.

These proportions should not be surprising. In fact, they only substantiate the observations which have already been made. The big urban centres have gained much more from the reforms than the more remote, rural and backward areas. Also the inhabitants of big urban agglomerations, due to their higher level of education and more 'dynamic' attitude to life, are much more open to any innovations and opportunities that may appear.

The above processes seem to form a clear pattern. The vast majority of Polish political elites are recruited from big urban centres. Their experience of recent reforms and their economic and social results are much more positive than those of 'ordinary people'. The level of optimism and approval of reforms is therefore much higher than from those who are paying the costs of the changes. It is therefore very likely that – even taking into account the fact that the new coalition came into power on the wave of criticism of too great a cost of reforms – their leaders will pursue the same course as their predecessors. This process, besides its economic rationale, also has a psychological justification which – in turn – has its roots in regional political profiles and elite recruitment mechanisms.

Some comment should be made about the local elections and local politics in Poland. As already mentioned above, the local elections of 1990 were of a 'plebiscite' type, i.e. the post-communist candidates were rejected in the majority of municipalities and the post-Solidarity political powers won these elections. However, the splits and conflicts within the Solidarity camps which began right after this event have not come down to the local level. The political divisions so strongly opposing each other on the national political scene were entirely absent from the local stage, because these parties were – in many cases – too small to have local institutions. Local politicians remained truly local, i.e. conflicts and tensions which emerged in the local councils were triggered by real local issues and personal conflicts, and in no way were the transmission of conflicts and tensions between the national parties. Local officials solved local problems in a pragmatic way, regardless of the political profiles these solutions might have.

This situation is likely to change dramatically very soon. The local elections ordered for spring 1994 have been much more politicised. The ruling coalition has retained its positions, while the opposition made an attempt to regain the support lost at the national level. However, the politicised elections have not produced politicised councils, at least in small localities, where everyday problems matter more than 'historical' processes of politics.

References

Berger, K. (1992) 'The state of natural environment.' In Zienkowski (ed) *op. cit.*

Central Planning Office (1993) *Raport o Polityce Regionalnej. Diagnoza (Report on the Regional Policy. Diagnosis)*. Warsaw: Central Planning Office.

Central Planning Office (1993) *The Concept of Development of International and Domestic Transport Connections*. Warsaw: Central Planning Office.

Central Planning Office (1994) *Raport o Polityce Regionalnej. Diagnoza (Report on Regional Policy. Diagnosis)*. Warsaw: Central Planning Office.

Central Statistical Office (1992) *Zatrudnienie i wynagrodzenia w gospodarce narodowej (Employment and wages in the national economy)*. Warsaw: Central Statistical Office.

Dziemianowicz, W. (1993) 'Foreign capital in Czechoslovakia, Hungary and Poland.' In G. Gorzelak and A. Kuklinski (eds) *Dilemmas of Regional Policies in Eastern and Central Europe*. Warsaw: EUROREG, vol. 8.

Gorzelak, G., Gieorgica, J.P., and Jalowiecki, B. (1992) *Case Study: Walbrzych 'Tourist Six.'* Brussels: Poland, Leda Report, European Commission.

Gorzelak, G., Kuklinski, A., Jalowiecki, B. and Zienkowski, L. (1994) 'Eastern and Central Europe 2000 – Final Report.' *Studies 2*. DGXII of the European Commission, Luxembourg.

Jalowiecki, B., Hryniewicz, J. and Mync, A. (1992) *Brain Drain from Polish Universities and Science*. Warsaw: EUROREG, vol.8.

Jalowiecki, B., Hryniewicz, J. and Mync, A. (1994) *Brain Drain from Polish Universities and Science 1992–1993*. Warsaw: EUROREG, vol.11.

Kornai, J. (1980) *Economics of Shortage*. Amsterdam: North Holland Publishing Company.

Maddox, B. (1994) 'Where the bison roam free.' Special Report: Poland, *Financial Times*, 18 March.64

Nesporova, A. and Kyloh, R. (1994) *Economic and Social Dialogue in the Ostrava-Karviná Region*. Budapest: ILO.

Robinson, A. 'Profile: Starachowice. Star-struck town fights back', Special Report: Poland, *Financial Times*, 18 March 1994.

Szul, R., Galazka, A. and Mync, A. (1993) *Warsaw as a Leader of Polish Transformation*. Warsaw: EUROREG.

Winiarski, B. (1993) 'Zachodnie regiony Polski – szanse i zagrozenia (Western Regions of Poland – chances and dangers).' Paper prepared for the project 'Restructuring of Polish Regions in an European Context. Wroclaw: EUROREG.

Zarycki, T. (1994) 'Profile polityczne wojewodztwa tarnobrzeskiego (Political profiles in Tarnobrzeg voivodship).' M.A. thesis, EUROREG.

Zienkowski, L. (ed) (1992) *Produkt krajowy brutto i dochody ludnosci welug wojewodztw w 1992 roku (Gross Domestic Product and Incomes of Population,* by Voivodships in 1992). Warsaw: GUS.

Zylicz, T. and Lehoczki, A. (1994) *Environmental Problems of the Four Countries in the Continental Framework,* prepared for the project 'Eastern and Central Europe 2000'.

Zylicz, T. and Spyrka, J. (1993) 'Towards environmental recovery – Poland.' Project report prepared within the 'East Central Europe 2000.' Stockholm/Warsaw.58

CHAPTER 4

The Regional Potential for Transformation

As has already been mentioned, just four years is too short a period for drawing final conclusions about the regional patterns of Polish transformation. However, the available data on both traditional differentiations of Polish space within its more general Central European context and the most recent processes of transformation prove one thing without any doubt: that in spite of dramatic changes in the Polish economy and Polish society, the general spatial structures of this country are stable.

The regions which have traditionally been mostly urbanised and mostly industrialised and which have been well equipped with infrastructure appear to be the least vulnerable to the costs and negative sides of transformation. They were able to proceed with privatisation at the fastest pace, to attract new (also foreign) investment and defend their position on the (changing) economic map of the country.[1] As a result, the traditional industrial-urban-infrastructural complex, which has shaped the regional structure of Poland has not vanished and has even been reinforced.

The strong became stronger, the weak became weaker. The polarisation effects, so visible in recent changes of economic and social structures, also manifest themselves in Polish space. It is almost certain that the growth of spatial differences will also take place in the future, since particular regions have developed – in the course of their history – differentiated potential for transformation and adaptation to new economic conditions. Only some regions of Poland will take advantage of new economic mechanism and internationalisation of Polish society and economy. For several others these new conditions lead to decline of their regional economies and create difficulties that will be hard to overcome during coming decade.

Summing up earlier remarks on economic, social and technological aspects of regional development of Poland, we may present the regional diversification of

---

1   The same result was found for the period of the previous Polish crisis 1976–1985, when the 'strongest' regions were stricken by crisis in the hardest way, but were the first to emerge from it and rebuild former structures.

Polish transformation along the following major dimensions of spatial differentiation, shaping the regions' ability to adapt to new economic conditions:

1. *Diversification of economic structure.* This dimension also includes the level and differentiation of skills of the workforce, and the modernity of fixed assets. In brief, the more diversified the economic structure, the more qualified the population will be and the level of technological advancement will be greater.

2. *Overall level of socio-economic development.* This dimension 'operates' on two levels: it discriminates rural areas (less developed) from towns, and the eastern part of the country (less developed) from the western part. It also captures the 'regional spirit' of entrepreneurship and the scale of job opportunities.

3. *Distance to sources of capital and innovation.* Several factors are of importance here: proximity to an international airport, proximity to the western border (i.e. to the German capital) and proximity to a big urban centre. 'The capital' is not only restricted to 'foreign capital', but also to domestic sources of finance, though the role of inflow of capital from abroad (and of new technologies) is of crucial importance for overall development of the Polish economy.

There are, of course, several other already-mentioned dimensions shaping the regional ability to transformation, like the agricultural structure, the density of 'company towns' with collapsing industry, vulnerability to the decline of eastern markets, ethnic tensions, etc. However, when looking into the chances of particular regions for their emergence from (often accidental) economic difficulties and their potential role in transforming Polish economy, the above three dimensions seem to be of primary importance.

Superimposition of these three dimensions produces a typology of Polish regions. This is presented in Table 4.1. Positions of a few voivodships in the table may be disputable. For example, three voivodships: Szczecin, Bielsko-Biala and Bydgoszcz may claim that they belong to group 1, which would be justified by the fast rate of privatisation, high involvement of foreign capital, proximity to international airports etc. However, these voivodships do not contain big urban centres with high scientific and cultural potential. Perhaps assigning some regions to group 2 (like Elblag and Leszno) could be considered as premature. One should also keep in mind that the potential of several regions is at the moment dominated by current difficulties. For example the region of Lódz may overcome its structural crisis caused by the collapse of the textile industry and join the regions of type 1. Similar remarks can also be made for several other individual cases. These reservations should not, however, overshadow the fact that Polish economic space is differentiated according to the three major factors which constitute the typology and that the spatial patterns, as presented in Table 4.1 (compare also Figure 4.1), do reflect the regions' potentialities for transformation.

Table 4.1 Typology of Polish regions from the point of view of their transformation potential

Types of regions	Regions	Socio-economic structure	Level of develop-ment	Proxim-ity to capital
Type 1: strong, leaders of transformation	Warsaw, Poznan, Wroclaw, Kraków, Gdansk	diversified	high	good
Type 2: well prepared for transform ation	Bydgoszcz, Torun, Szczecin, Gorzów, Zielona Góra, Kalisz, Opole, Bielsko-Biala, Lublin, Leszno, Elblag	diversified	medium	good
Type 3: restructuring needed, poss-ible	Jelenia Góra, Legnica, Pila, Koszalin, Siupsk, Olsztyn, Tarnobrzeg, Tarnów, Kielce, Czestochowa, Bialystok, Rzeszów, Plock	diversified with company-towns	medium/ low	bad
Type 4: deep restruc-turing necess-ary, difficult	Katowice, Lódz, Walbrzych	diversified, monofunctional (industrial)	high	good/ medium
Type 5: presenting some potential for develop-ment	Suwalki, Ciechanów, Ostroieka, Lomza, Biala-Podlaska, Chelm, Zamosc, Przemysl, Krosno	monofunctional (agricultural)	low	bad
Type 6: neutral, some sectors need restructuring	Konin, Piotrków, Sieradz, Wloclawek, Skierniewice, Radom, Nowy Sacz, Siedlce	diversified	medium	medium

Source: Gorzelak (1993)

Let us therefore summarise – sometimes also providing some new information – the situation of particular regions of Poland after three years of transformation. This summary will also lead to sketching the chances of particular regions for the coming years.

1. *Warsaw, Poznan, Kraków, Wroclaw, Gdansk and, to some extent, Szczecin, are without doubt the leaders in Polish transformation.* Unemployment is low, job opportunities much more numerous than elsewhere. The labour force is well educated, the infrastructure relatively well developed. These cities concentrate a vast share of Polish scientific and academic potential. Privatisation processes are the fastest, inflow of foreign capital the greatest, growth of the service sector the most rapid. The economic situation of these regions seems promising, with the possible exception of Kraków, in which the future of huge steel mill, Nowa Huta (employing over 20,000 persons), is uncertain.

   These regions will concentrate the main bulk of Polish recovery and will become the nodes of technological progress, economic efficiency and cultural advancement.

It should be envisaged that the growth rate of all these regions will well exceed the national average in the time horizon covered by this analysis. It can reach up to 10% yearly, with the fastest growth in the service sector (especially in Warsaw itself), high-tech industries and specialised manufacturing.

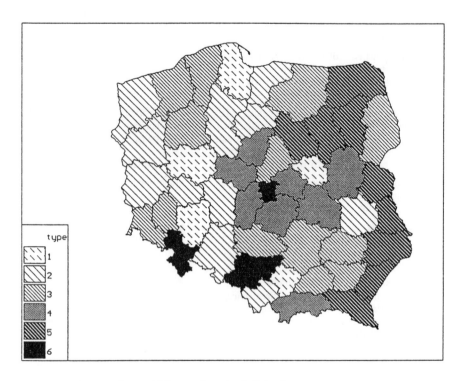

Figure 4.1 The regional potential for transformation in Poland

2. Typical *old industrial regions* constitute another regional pattern in Poland. These are *Upper Silesia* (see next point), *Lódz* and *Walbrzych* regions. In the case of Lódz it is the textile industry and in the Walbrzych region coal mining and textile industries which have constituted the economic base in the past and have almost collapsed. The traditional Soviet market for textiles has virtually closed down and coal have been almost totally extracted from the Walbrzych pits (only a few of them have been closed). Devising promising development strategy is difficult due the monofunctional qualification structure of the local workforce, the polluted environment, the worn-down infrastructure and – in the Walbrzych region – the exploited natural resources. In some parts of the Walbrzych region tourism seems to be the most promising direction for local development.

There is a marked difference between Lódz and Walbrzych. *Lódz is a typical 'great city' region*, which demonstrates all the advantages of an urban agglomeration. It concentrates a well-educated labour force, and scientific and academic institutions. It is centrally located in the country and its location advantages will even increase with the construction of two highways, north–south and east–west. Privatisation processes are relatively fast and the involvement of foreign capital visible. Services develop rapidly. However, the old dominant industry, now being in a really difficult situation, is a heavy burden for this region. The massive unemployment, over-representation of narrowly educated workers and the worn-down urban infrastructure jeopardise the chances of this city for taking full advantage of its potential for transformation.

Walbrzych is in a much more difficult position. This region has all the features of an old industrial region and does not have the potential of a big city. Its location is not advantageous. Having said that, one should not forget about the tourist potential concentrated in the southern part of the region, which may be a great chance for some communes and towns.

It is inevitable for the Walbrzych region to go through a period of decline. With the exception of tourism, all other sectors do not demonstrate any potential for growth. Lódz seems to be in a better position, since the potential of this region may be well utilised. However, it is unlikely for the Lódz region to exceed the average national rate of growth, since the declining industries will be – for several years – a heavy burden for its economy.

3. *Upper Silesia* of which the Katowice voivodship constitutes the main part and the major economic unit, traditionally providing more than 20% of the national industrial production, is on the edge of massive restructuring and dramatic increase of unemployment. Coal mining, the most important branch in the regional economy, will undergo deep structural changes. Heavy and chemical industries, being at the moment in decline, are the other dominating sectors of Upper Silesia and will produce massive unemployment in the near future. For example, the programme of coal mining restructuring envisaged closing down 14–17 coal mines and a reduction of employment in this economic sector by 170,000 people. Five steel mills in the region are to be closed in the same time-horizon, which will lead to the dismissal of a further 30,000 workers. Further reductions of employment will take place in factories co-operating with those which are to be liquidated.

However, *until now the true restructuring process seems to have not started yet in the region*. Production of coal dropped by more than 30%, while employment in this branch has declined by less than 15% (together with energy production). Polish coal becomes more expensive than that on the world markets, but its production is still relatively high, though the deficit of the coal mines grows by 50 million US dollars monthly. During the years 1990 and 1992 the overall industrial employment dropped down by 45,000 people and in construction grew in the same period by 27,000. The more postponed the adjustment of employment in the region will be, the more massive reductions will have to be made and higher social costs will be paid.

The economic profile of Upper Silesia can no longer be maintained and possibilities of building new industrial structures even on the ruins of the old are vague. The environment is too heavily damaged, the labour force too monofunctional, infrastructure too obsolete, society too critical. In the meantime, the rate of unemployment in the Katowice and Bielsko-Biala voivodships is one of the lowest in Poland, which – as explained above – should not be the case in the future.

At the same time, both voivodships seem to benefit from the transformation processes. Upper Silesia is one of the leading regions in privatisation and inflow of foreign capital. In the Bielsko-Biala voivodship the biggest foreign investment in Poland was located – FIAT, with up to 2 billion USD committed for next years. The situation of these two regions is therefore, to some extent, 'broken': they take advantage of a relatively well-developed infrastructure and the 'big city' effects, and, at the same time, the shadow of industrial restructuring and its social costs may jeopardise – especially in the Katowice region – the course of transformation.

It is a paradoxical phenomenon that Polish political elites seem to try very hard to forget about Upper Silesia. The problems of restructuring the two other regions; Lódz and Walbrzych, have much greater coverage in mass-media and meet with greater attention from the government. This was, however, only the result of the Silesian strike in December 1992 when this region came to the fore, just for a while. The Silesian problem – especially difficult economically, socially and politically – is being pushed out of the consciousness of the decision-making centres. The consequences may be dramatic, since postponing any action – action which far exceeds present and future capabilities of the Polish economy – aggravates the Silesian problem.

Upper Silesia will be the region in sharp recession for the coming years. Once the real restructuring starts, several leading industries will have to note deep decline of their output which would not be able to be compensated by the growth of progressive branches. The negative rate of growth seems to be the fate of this region for the next decade.

4. The *central-western regions* (Wielkopolska) and their extension to the north
    and to the south – i.e. the territories which constitute the 'letter L' – are
    now and will be in the future the greatest beneficiaries of the
    transformation processes, along with the big cities mentioned in point 1.
    These are the areas with diversified economic structure, rich endowment
    with infrastructure (which will be further enhanced by the north–south
    highway), well-developed urban system, high level of agricultural
    productivity and advantageous location.

    The entrepreneurial spirit and long traditions of good organisation are the
    main assets of the Wielkopolska region. By all standards, these areas will
    play a crucial role in Polish transformation as an immediate background to
    the leading cities listed in point 1.

    The 'letter L' areas of Poland will demonstrate growth similar to the
    national averages. The non-agricultural sectors will display faster growth;
    however, the important position of agriculture in their economies will pull
    this rate down.

5. *The north eastern part of Poland (voivodships: Olsztyn, Suwalki, Lomza, Ostroleka,
    Ciechanów)* is one of the regions in which transformation may be slower.
    This is the region most endangered by structural unemployment. The
    non-agricultural sectors are poorly developed and employment
    opportunities other than in agriculture are scarce. Agriculture itself is rather
    weak, poorly equipped with fixed capital and run by elderly farmers with
    low skills and little incentive. Tourist services cannot develop properly due
    to a general decrease of incomes and low demand for such services. The
    region creates limited opportunities for potential foreign investors due to
    its remoteness and overall economic, social and cultural backwardness.
    Links with the eastern markets are still poor and do not create hopes for
    revitalising local economy.

    The north eastern part of Poland may perhaps adapt its role to play at the
    international level as one of the few European reservoirs of *unspoiled
    environment*. Conflicts between tourist services and environmental functions
    are possible.

6. *The south eastern part of Poland* has a concentration of '*company-towns*' hosting
    declining branches, such as the metallurgic, military and transportation
    industries which are in a difficult economic situation. The collapse of the
    former Soviet market to which this region directed a great share of its
    industrial production has been one of the most important factors of present
    economic difficulties. This region also had a concentration of the
    'bi-professionals' who combined their work in industry with running a
    small agricultural farm. They were the first to be dismissed from their
    industrial occupation, but the remaining source of maintenance – farming –
    is usually too small to provide a sufficient income. The urban structure is

relatively well developed but it might undergo accelerated deterioration along with worsening of the economic situation of the state industrial enterprises which used to construct and support the communal facilities. Other directions of development are limited: agriculture is (traditionally) heavily overpopulated and tourist services are underdeveloped. Trade with new eastern markets could be the direction of regional specialisation in the future, though this depends on developments in the post-Soviet republics.

Especially dramatic changes may occur in agriculture. For centuries this region has had the smallest land holdings and, at the same time, a relatively low agricultural culture. This will be the region in which eventually the greatest numbers of people will be pushed out of agricultural jobs. However, due to relative backwardness, the local market for agricultural services may be limited and in this way these people will have great difficulties in finding non-agricultural occupations in the rural areas. Thus, rural unemployment may sore, adding to the already massive urban unemployment.

The very south eastern corner of Poland may play a similar role as a reservoir of natural environment.

7. *Northern and western Polish regions* have a specific agricultural structure: the share of state and co-operative farms was the highest and reached, in some regions, over 50% of agricultural land. These big farms collapsed and were put for privatisation, which is slow due to a lack of demand for buying land. Though unemployment created as the result of restructuring of this economic sector is not great by absolute numbers, it can strongly influence some local labour markets deprived of other employment opportunities.

   The already discussed prospects for internationalisation of this region – especially of its western part – may solve some of these problems. However, the inflow of foreign (in fact German) capital will not create a sufficient number of jobs in the near future. The labour market will therefore be one of the most difficult problems for these territories for at next few years.

   Tourist services will constitute an important developmental factor for the seaside. However, the benefits of this type of economic activity will be limited to the 5–10 kms belt along the coast and the multiplier effects will not embrace the more distant hinterland.

   These last three groups of regions (points 5–7) will – in general – fall into the group of losers. Their rates of growth will be lower than the national averages, though some particular regions may also reach the higher dynamics of economic development.

8. Besides these more general regional patterns of Poland, there are several cases of micro-regions which will pose specific developmental problems. The most pronounced will be the restructuring processes of some

raw-material extraction and processing centres, like the copper-mining
basin in Legnica and Lubin (south west), the sulphur basin around
Tarnobrzeg (south east), the brown coal mining and energy producing
centres near Konin (central-west) and Turoszów (south west corner) etc.
These are the regions deeply endangered by low profitability of production
(copper, sulphur) and by environmental hazards. Their production will have
to decrease and this will lead to the emergence of geographically
concentrated social and economic depressions.

In more general terms, it is becoming clear that all four countries have their
unquestionable *leaders of transformation*, which have already demonstrated the
highest potential for restructuring and a great capability for adaptation to new
conditions. These are their greatest agglomerations: *Prague and Brno in the Czech
Republic; Bratislava and to a lesser extent Kosice in Slovakia; Budapest and the Balaton region
in Hungary; already indicated, Warsaw, Poznan, Wroclaw, Gdansk and Kraków in Poland.*

However, some of these nodes are not surrounded by an innovative and
progressive hinterland. Warsaw is a kind of island within a relatively poorly
developed central part of Poland. Kraków borders on the west a very difficult (if
not the most difficult) regional case in Europe (Upper Silesia) and on the east the
Polish south eastern periphery. Kosice is a relatively small urban centre in backward
eastern Slovakia.

On the other hand, the space between the remaining nodes is filled in by the
regions which are in fact the core areas of all four Central European countries.
These regions for centuries have concentrated the main bulk of development and
innovation. They have also proved to be natural candidates to become the final
winners of transformation.

We have sketched in this way the *core of Central Europe: 'the Central European
boomerang' delimited by the following centres: Gdansk–Poznan–Wroclaw–Prague–Brno–
Bratislava/Vienna–Budapest. Two southern parts of this 'boomerang' have real chances to
become the truly European centres: the region of Prague and the triangle composed of
Vienna–Bratislava–Budapest.* The Slovak–Hungarian part of this triangle already
attracts important foreign capital flowing into Central Europe and the location
advantages of this region have been evaluated as extremely favourable even on the
continental scale (see Figure 4.2).

Further extension of the Prague region westwards is very probable, since the
construction of motorways connecting Prague with southern Germany and Berlin
will bring multiplier effects and will create favourable conditions for economic
expansion. It will allow for full integration of Prague into the system of European
metropoles.

Warsaw is located peripherally to this core of Central Europe. However, as an
over 2 million agglomeration and a capital of an almost 40 mn nation, it will retain
its role as a European city of the second order. It is quite probable that if the
restructuring of the Lódz agglomeration is successful (and there are good chances
for it, since Lódz, besides its industry, also presents rich potential as an academic

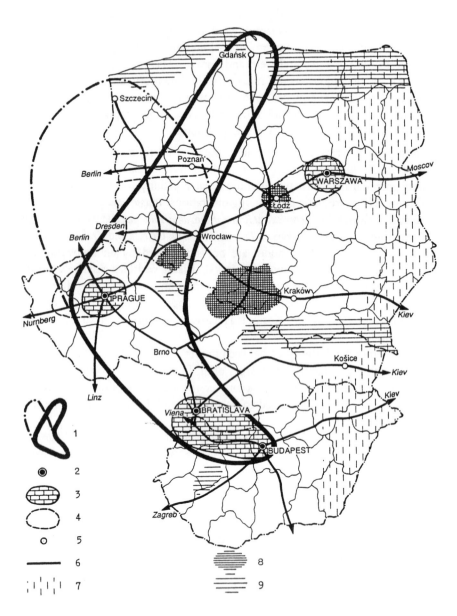

Notes: 1) present and potential Central European axes; 2) major centres of
transformation; 3) cores of transformation; 4) potential cores of transformation;
5) centres of transformation; 6) main existing or projected highways; 7)
Central European 'eastern wall'; 8) old industrial regions 9) regions with
tourist potential

Source: Gorzelak *et al.* (1994)

Figure 4.2 The Central European 'boomerang' – a concentration of transformation processes

and medical centre) a core area will be created by these two agglomerations. The same applies to the extension of the Poznan agglomeration westwards, along the international route Paris–Moscow (the existing expressway already attracts many services and other economic activities).

The southern part of the 'Central European boomerang' seems to be more integrated internally and externally with wider Europe. The northern part, from Poznan to Gdansk, lacks sufficient infrastructure and transportation connections (there are no motorways planned to connect Gdansk with Poznan). It is therefore very likely that the present shape of the 'boomerang', which expresses the current core of the higher level of development and prospected dynamics of economic activity, will be changed and pulled westwards by the growing role of *Berlin* which is very likely to soon assume the role of a European metropolis of the first order (together with London and Paris). The 'boomerang' will then become a 'foot', embracing Berlin and Szczecin instead of extending north to Gdansk. The traditional transport connections from the Czech Republic to the Baltic Sea through the Szczecin-Swinoujscie harbour and the planned highway from Szczecin to Budapest might add new factors to this shape with accelerated development. Successful integration of the former East Germany into the wide German economic-spatial system will no doubt create more favourable grounds for this process.

There are two 'black holes' in the socio-economic space of Central Europe: the Silesia and Lódz regions. Both of them have already been commented upon.

Central Europe has a very clearly marked *periphery*. It extends from the north eastern corner of Poland to the south eastern part of Hungary, with extension westwards to the eastern part of the Slovak–Hungarian border. These are the least developed, relatively sparsely populated rural areas with poorly developed urban system and infrastructure. These areas are crossed by main transportation routes going in the east–west direction and no major artery exists or is envisaged which would connect them in the north–south direction. All of these regions are poorly integrated with the centres of their respective national systems. Transformation processes are slow there, the level of education low and they do not attract the attention of foreign investors (the Hungarian regions could be the only exception).

What is even more important from the prospective point of view, is that these areas cannot expect to receive inducement for transformation and recovery from their neighbours on the other side of the border (Lithuania, Byelorussia, Ukraine). Even if the scenario of chaos and permanent recession in these post-Soviet republics is ruled out, there are no serious chances that the trans-border co-operation could create any important impulses for growth and modernisation. Moreover, since the economic power of the *Central European eastern wall* is very limited, there is no indigenous capital which could take advantage of the existence of the market behind the eastern border. These opportunities, if taken at all, will benefit the more prosperous core regions of Central Europe and the West. *It is therefore very likely that the eastern wall will become the 'dead end' of Central Europe.*

There are a few more regions which demonstrate promising chances for development and which could be more visible even on a European scale. These are the regions which are the *European reservoirs of unspoiled environment.* North east of Poland and the entire border region of Poland and Slovakia do create very promising chances for becoming the basins for tourist services and recreation on a continental scale, providing that these functions will not damage the purest nature in Europe, since conflicts between tourist services and environmental functions are possible. The shore of the Baltic Sea might also have chances for attracting tourists. The same applies to the tourist recreational and spa centres with long traditions, like the west Bohemia spa triangle of Karlovy Vary–Marianske Lázne–Frantiskovy Lázne, the north western spa region of Poland in the Walbrzych voivodship (Polanica–Kudowa–Duszniki) and the Balaton Lake region in Hungary.

The majority of these areas lack sufficient tourist infrastructure, if not in quantitative terms then certainly in qualitative. Development and upgrading of this infrastructure so that it could meet the requirements of more demanding customers is the crucial condition for these regions if their chances are not to be missed. More intensified co-operation between Poland and Slovakia seems also to be a condition for the development of their tourist border regions.

Besides these more general regional patterns of Central Europe, there are several cases of micro-regions which will pose specific developmental problems. The most pronounced will be the restructuring processes of some raw-material extraction and processing centres. These are the regions deeply endangered by low profitability of production (uranium, lignite, copper, sulphur, heavy metal-lurgy) and by environmental hazards. Their production will have to decrease and this will lead to the emergence of very geographically concentrated social and economic depressions.

References

Gorzelak, G. (1993) *Poland 2005: The Regional Scenario.* Warsaw: EUROREG.

Gorzelak, G., Kuklinski, A., Jalowiecki, B. and Zienkowski, L. (1994) 'Eastern and Central Europe 2000 – Final Report.' *Studies 2.* DGXII of the European Commission, Luxembourg.

CHAPTER 5

Regional Policies

Lack of National Regional Policies

There are at least four governmental agencies in Poland responsible for formulating and implementing 'regional' or 'spatial' policies in either an explicit or implicit way. The Department of Physical and Long-Term Planning of the Central Planning Office (CPO) is supposed to formulate perspective economic and physical plans for Poland and to establish foundations for state regional policy. The Ministry for Physical Planning and Construction is responsible for urban planning and physical planning on the local level as well as for new regulations concerning land use, ownership of land, building standards, etc. The department of the Council of Ministers Office deals with the regional governmental authorities and the territorial organisation of the state. Finally, the Ministry of Finance deals with the financial aspects of local governments.

It has to be openly stated that neither of these bodies has formulated a progressive, offensive regional/spatial national policy.

The CPO puts forward proposals for regional state policy which are based on defensive assumptions, oriented towards reacting to processes and phenomena that have already emerged (like unemployment) instead of forecasting the processes that will take place and provide an adequate regional/spatial framework for them. It has been very often stated that for at least two and a half decades there has been no regional (spatial) policy in Poland. According to the documents of the CPO:[1]

> During the first phase of transformation the priorities of the macroeconomic policy of the state have greatly limited any possibilities for conducting the sectoral of regional policies. Especially, the implementation of the 'shock therapy' during the first half of 1990 has not allowed to break the rules of the game. (p.39)

---

1   Central Planing Office 1994a and Central Planing Office 1994b.

This statement gives the impression that this *limitation* was the necessary objective. In fact, this is disputable, since very many critics of the shock therapy applied in Poland indicate that some sectoral programmes should have been implemented, at the expense, of course, of the 'pure' doctrine of non-intervention of the state into the economic processes – which, in reality, has often been broken.

The first signs of any reaction of the state to the growing spatial differences in reactions of particular regions to the transformation processes were concentrated in the Walbrzych region, the first and – at that time, i.e. already in 1990 – the most pronounced recession region in Poland. The case of Lódz was the next one to attract the attention of institutions responsible for regional policies. In fact, their interventionist approach dominated all declarations of these institutions and their actions – as weak as these were. The report states explicitly:

> The practical realisation of the goals of the state regional policy has been shaped by the pressure exerted by the regions most affected by the social consequences of restructuring. Since the trade unions acted as the exponents of these consequences, this pressure was closely related to the strength of the regional structures of the trade unions. This in turn was responsible for the fact that the 'old industrial regions' have dominated the 'rural regions with low incomes' (*op. cit.*, p.42).

The quoted report specifies the state subsidies which have been granted to particular regions in consecutive years. In all three years 1991–1993 these have been allocated to the infrastructure creation in regions most endangered by structural unemployment. However, these funds were, in fact, negligible, since they constituted 0.17, 0.16 and 0.10 per cent of the state budget spending in respective years (i.e. ten times less than in highly developed countries). The decreasing share proves how unimportant regional policy is in the eyes of those who are responsible for the Polish economy.

The Ministry of Finance directs the general subsidies to local budgets. An 'objective' formula is in use, according to which these funds are being allocated to particular municipalities. The formula, which is based on the size of population, generally does not take any account of the structural differences between particular localities, i.e. a tiny rural commune would be treated in a similar way to a big city. Some derivation from the general principles have been in use before 1994 and made some allowance for the size of town; some specific functions, like tourist resort, border crossing, sea harbour; environmental conditions; quality of soils; employment structure dominated by agriculture; finally, Warsaw was supported due to its function as the state capital. Since the beginning of 1994 no such exemptions from the general formula were applied, which ruined any possibility of any type of regional policy.

The role of the Ministry of Physical Planning and Construction has been limited to influencing the fiscal aspects of the construction sector and the general building and physical planning rules. This ministry is very reluctant to look beyond the local level and does not intend to play an active role on a regional scale.

The role of the Councils' of Ministers Office is most marked in two spheres: the political composition of the regional authorities and the pace of the reforms of the territorial organisation of the state, and the relations of the governmental and self-governmental authorities on the sub-regional levels. These issues will be discussed elsewhere in this book. It is enough to mention here that this particular governmental agency does not conduct any economic or social regional policy.

In this situation, in which there is no governmental institution which would specify the principles of the regional policy of the state and which would be strong enough to influence all other governmental bodies so that the policies would be congruent with these principles, the *sectoral policies* seem to exert the strongest influence on the regional processes. These are, however, only two examples of an explicit regional policy conducted by a sectoral ministry: the Ministry of Labour and Social Policy, and the Ministry of Environment and Natural Resources.

The first of these two, all of a sudden, emerged as the governmental agency with the strongest inputs into regional policies. This ministry deals with severe cases of structural unemployment, which leads this ministry to being involved in regional/local intervention.

The first feature which makes the Ministry of Labour and Social Policy exceptional is the fact that it delimits areas structurally endangered by unemployment and it differentiates its policies according to this delimitation. The *employment policy* is the only one which uses special areas on which some economic instruments are used.

Already in 1990 regions with high structural unemployment were identified. Along the course of rapid growth of unemployment further areas have been added. On 24 August 1992 the Council of Ministers approved a new list of 245 municipalities especially endangered by unemployment, which was further extended in August 1993 to 412 units. These municipalities occupy 22 per cent of the country's area and are inhabited by some 15 per cent of the total population of Poland and concentrate more than 20 per cent of the total number of unemployed. The majority of these areas have noted a rate of unemployment twice as high as the national average.

The regional coverage follows the old pattern, which, obviously, closely corresponds to the spatial distribution of unemployment in Poland. The municipalities especially endangered by unemployment are located in 26 voivodships. Two industrial voivodships, Walbrzych and Lódz, and one region with rural unemployment caused by the collapse of state farms, Slupsk, are entirely covered by these areas. In three other regions of this last type (Suwalki, Olsztyn and Koszalin) almost the entire territory has been assigned to this category.

A new category has been recently created: these are the areas in which unemployment grows rapidly. There are 18 such areas located in 13 voivodships (Bielsko-Biala, Bydgoszcz, Ciechanów, Jelenia Góra, Kielce, Legnica, Lublin, Nowy Sacz, Plock, Radom, Szczecin, Tarnobrzeg, Zielona Góra).

The municipalities endangered by structural unemployment, located in these regions, enjoy the following measures and incentives:

1. Accelerated amortisation rates of fixed assets bought after 1 January 1991. The enterprises are allowed to calculate amortisation according to the highest rates, which should create resources for new investment and new job creation.

2. Infrastructural grants from the state budget which will go to the local budget and will allow for infrastructure development, in this way creating new jobs.

3. Income tax reliefs for private businesses which run vocational training and re-training and a right to exceed the limit of employment without paying higher taxes.

4. Firms which employ graduates of vocational, secondary and university-level schools who have been directed by the Employment Offices are exempted from the compulsory payments to the Work Fund and from income and salary taxes for a period of 12 months.

5. A right to business with foreign capital higher than 2 million Ecu to apply to the Ministry of Finance for income tax reliefs. The enterprises introducing new technologies and declaring exports of at least 20 per cent of their production will have preference. Up to now only five such firms have been granted the reductions.

6. Grants from the Work Fund for active forms of coping with unemployment.

It has to be admitted, however, that this is – obviously – only one element of regional development and regional policy. Moreover, the doctrine adopted by this ministry is – perhaps necessarily – one-sided. It is oriented towards 'assisting the poor and the weak' and any assistance for 'the good and the strong' (which becomes a more and more pronounced doctrine of modern regional policies) is not present in activities of this particular ministry.

Until now there is no comprehensive evaluation of the efficiency of these measures and incentives. The Ministry of Finance does not collect information on accelerated amortisation. The Ministry of Labour and Social Policy collects data on granted loans and expenditure on infrastructure development, but is not able to evaluate the effects of such measures. In this light the measures and incentives applied on a local level in order to alleviate unemployment function, to some extent, 'in a mist'.

There are also a few other instruments of regional policy in Poland, related to the *environment protection*. These are:

1. Fees for water used for other purposes than production of energy. The fees are increased by a factor of five in the following voivodships: Bielsko-Biala, Czestochowa, Jelenia Góra, Kielce, Kraków, Legnica, Nowy Sacz, Opole, Tarnów, Walbrzych and Wroclaw. For the Katowice voivodships these fees are increased by 100 per cent.

2. There are special (restrictive) norms of air pollution for some areas – nature reserves, national parks, health resorts etc.

There have been attempts to cope with specific, 'problem' regions. In two cases the Governmental Representatives have been nominated for regional restructuring: one (within the structure of the Ministry of Labour and Social Policy) for the Walbrzych region and another (in February 1993) for the Lódz region. A plan of regional restructuring has been formulated which included statements on the magnitude and time-table of closing coal pits and social allowances for the released employees. This plan is based on state funds. Until now the effects are rather limited and intensity of activities low.

Policies of Regions

Regional authorities – being a part of the central governmental administration – do not conduct their own policies as such. This does not mean, however, that they are entirely indifferent towards the process ongoing in their regions. Several types of activities may be mentioned:

1. *Claiming funds and assistance from the central government.* This seems to be one of the most commonly used 'regional policies', though it does not appear to be the most successful *vis-à-vis* restrictive monetary policies of all consecutive Polish governments.

2. Organising *regional councils, foundations for regional restructuring etc.*, which should co-ordinate actions and efforts undertaken by several institutions and agencies on the regional level (for example, such a foundation was organised in the Walbrzych region). This type of policy may be useful as a mobilising factor of local elites and local economic agents.

3. Creating *regional development agencies.* By the end of 1994 there were over 50 regional development agencies in Poland, almost evenly distributed in the country.[2] These agencies should be self-supporting. Initial capital is collected from share-holders (or, exceptionally, founders) and the state (represented by the Agency of Industrial Development) may contribute up to 40 per cent of its value. Regional/local development agencies are created in areas endangered by structural unemployment which have acute economic restructuring problems. The agencies aim at creating new jobs

---

2 See Langota and Walen (1992)

which would replace jobs lost during the restructuring processes, active utilisation of local potential and development of institutional structures which would combine national and local efforts and actions undertaken within the process of economic restructuring.

Agencies are created mainly by the regional administration and by local authorities. There is a whole array of institutions supporting these agencies, such as business associations and clubs, chambers of commerce and industry, banks, agencies of local initiatives etc. The agencies perform (or at least are supposed to perform) the following activities:

- assistance in preparation of local/regional development strategies; for this purpose agencies should possess comprehensive data files on local economic units and their potential partners, as well thorough knowledge of rules, regulations and strategies of central authorities;

- consultancy services for local economic units (state-owned, private, municipal) aiming at promotion of entrepreneurship and efficiency; educational services should be offered by the agencies;

- financial operations and co-operation with banks; agencies evaluate business plans forwarded by firms applying for credit; they locate their funds in banks and enter into partnerships with businesses; they also guarantee loans for recommended applications.

There is no comprehensive evaluation of existing regional/local development agencies. However, several experiences are really encouraging. They have become, in some instances, real partners for local authorities and have contributed to local/regional development of the area they operate on. In five regions (Lódz, Walbrzych, Rzeszów, Suwalki-Olsztyn and Katowice) the agencies are responsible for implementing programmes within the STRUDER fund, a three-year, 60 million ECU programme within the PHARE framework.

The reforms of the territorial organisation of the state will further reinforce the powers of both local and regional levels. In particular, the 12–14 regions (and not 25, as some propose) will enable the regional units to conduct their own regional policies, within the framework of the guidelines provided by the state.

The Role of Local Government in Local Development

In mature democracies local government plays an important role in local development. Polish local governments, for several reasons, seem to be much less active in this sphere. According to a survey conducted in 1991[3] local authorities are not involved in promoting the local economy. Very often they do not even have sufficient information about the current number of firms, their activities, needs and problems. Lack of information makes any active local policy (taxation, rents, infrastructure development etc.) virtually impossible and even these limited possibilities which are at the disposal of local authorities are not fully utilised.

The survey revealed that local authorities (represented in the research by mayors and presidents of local councils) were not aware of how the growth of private local services may contribute to local development. On average, in their opinions only 'better satisfaction of social needs' could be achieved in this way and such factors as tax revenue, mobilisation of local community by good example, rents from communal property and job creation were considered by them as of minor importance. Regional differentiation could be noticed: in Wielkopolska job creation was considered as an element of major importance (and this is the region with the greatest unemployment problems). Representatives of towns perceived the local private sphere as more important than local authorities from remote rural areas. Very few representatives of local governments asked, considered privatisation of municipal services as important for the local economy.

This consciousness of major actors within local government was in opposition to the needs of local private businessmen. They did expect to receive some assistance from local authorities in the form of local financial incentives, development of technical infrastructure, efficient administrative services, external promotion of the local economy etc. Owners and managers of bigger firms perceived local authorities as a kind of shelter in their disputes and conflicts with central and regional institutions.

Observation of local systems reveal that the role of local business communities is growing in importance on the local social, economic and political scene. In these local units which have a relatively well-developed private sphere, local businessmen have entered local elites and are able to influence decision-making processes.

Local authorities do not have any real powers to interfere with the fate of state enterprises located on their territory. These enterprises are directly subordinated either to appropriate ministry or to regional administration and all decisions are

---

3   The survey was conducted in June 1991 in 104 purposely selected municipalities located in ten voivodships. It was directed to the representatives of local economy (private and state enterprises) and to local authorities. For an extensive report on results see Jalowiecki (1992)

made in 'vertical' lines, with almost entire omission of local government. Local authorities may only exert indirect pressure. As a result, decisions which may seriously affect local units are made externally.

What are the reasons for this limited involvement of local authorities in promoting local development on their territories? Several factors can be mentioned:

1. Limited formal and real competencies of local government. Local budgets constitute only some 14–15 per cent of the entire state budget. Local taxes are low and therefore cannot be used by local authorities as an active tool for influencing behaviour of local economic agents. Local governments are too much restricted by general regulations in several spheres of their activity (e.g. privatising municipal property, rents). In the majority of localities there are several establishments which are managed by external authorities (entire enterprises, property of enterprises located elsewhere) following their own rules and interests, thus often breaking the logic of local development.

2. Limited skills of local authorities in such crucial fields, like planning local economic development, administrative services for local businesses, municipal marketing, promotion, etc.

3. General underdevelopment of institutions which should serve both local goverments and firms, such as banks (communal banks are virtually non-existent), consultancy firms of different kinds (several existing consultancies are oriented towards easy money and do not present sufficient knowledge), advertising agencies, educational and training institutions etc.

4. Pressure of everyday matters at the expense of longer term planning and reflection on long-run developmental problems of a given locality (this is, however, a general problem of Polish authorities at all levels).

There is, probably, no possibility of applying any short-cut methods which would alleviate these difficulties and heal deficiencies all of a sudden. However, several actions might be undertaken and sometimes have already been undertaken to accelerate general educational efforts and the development of necessary institutions.

Since several local tasks cannot be performed by a single local authority, the creation of inter-municipal associations has accelerated in Poland during recent years.[4]

---

4   See Michalak (1992)

In 1992 there were 56 such associations in Poland. They can be divided into three groups:

1. associations aiming at joint solving all or some problems of the municipal economy (29 associations);

2. associations performing public tasks along with some economic activity and representing their members in external contacts (with central and regional authorities, potential economic partners etc. – 22 associations);

3. associations created for the sake of environmental protection and coping with pollution and nature degradation (5 associations).

As in the case of the regional development agencies, no comprehensive report on the performances and results achieved by the inter-municipal association is available. Some occasional evidence shows, however, that several such cases should lead their members to success.

Subsidies of the state budget to the municipal budgets are estimated on the basis of strict criteria, which take into account basic features of the local units. Until 1993 these subsidies were increased if a given municipality fulfilled one (or more) of the following conditions:

- was a town of more than 100,000 inhabitants;
- had on its territory a spa, sea harbour or a border crossing;
- was located in an area of special environmental quality;
- was located in an area with severe ecological problems;
- had poor quality soils;
- was a capital;
- had more than 70 per cent of its population's incomes derived from agriculture and forestry.

These criteria did not take into account any wider regional setting of the municipalities. After 1993 only the size of the municipality influenced the amount of subsidy – towns with a population of over 300,000 received 1.5 more per inhabitant than municipalities with 5000 or less. In any case, therefore, these measures cannot be regarded as a measure of the regional policy of the state.

Reform of the Territorial Organisation of the State

The present territorial organisation of Polish space is generally considered as inadequate to new economic and political conditions.

First of all, the regional (voivodship) unit is much too small for the new type of regional policy that should be designed and implemented by the central government. *The Polish administrative regions of the first-order should be visible on the map of Europe* and such units should be strong enough to conduct their own development policies and to be economically competitive, even in the international context. The development of the technical infrastructure, necessary for creating favourable conditions for the foreign capital intending to invest in Poland, is another task of the national regional policy, which calls for bigger spatial units being able to undertake such tasks.

Second, the old '*powiat*' (district) is still visible on the economic map of Poland. Social infrastructure (schools, hospitals, cultural establishments etc.) do still exist in some 300 medium-sized towns which used to be the district capitals. The same applies to the public transport infrastructure.

Third, the proceeding process of 'municipalisation' of the state, i.e. of transferring several new responsibilities from the central government to self-government, calls for the creation of bigger self-governmental units. Present municipalities appear to be too small and too weak to undertake such broader responsibilities.

All these reasons support the proposed reform, according to which some 12–14 regional units[5] and some 300 districts should be created in Poland. This reform is currently being prepared and discussed. However, several problems are still to be solved. These are the following:

1. The constitutional status of new regions. All solutions between the two extremes: full autonomy (federalisation of the country) and full subordination to the central government were proposed. This issue will be discussed below.

2. The division of competence between the self-government of municipalities and districts.

3. The timing of reform. The district boundaries will cross the voivodship frontiers which means that both new types of territorial units should be introduced at the same time. However, since this reform will mean such a distortion to the entire country, it is disputable if it should be introduced soon, before other – economic, social and political – problems are settled.

One of the quite reasonable delimitations of the possible new big regions of Poland is presented in Figure 5.1.[6]

In regard to the constitutional status of the new, big regions, four models of regionalisation in Poland,[7] which can be applied during the proposed reform, have been distinguished:

---

5   A full well-documented account of the concept of creating 12 big regions was given by Wysocka and Kozinski (1993)

6   There are also other proposals for the shape of new voivodships. The creation of 25 regions is one of these solutions challenging the model of 12.

Source: Wysocka and Kozinski (1993)

Figure 5.1 Proposed new big voivodships in Poland

1. *Regional deconcentration* of the central authority. Regional authority (*voivod*) represents the prime minister. The voivodship does not have legal entity – all regional administration is, in fact, a part of the governmental system. Self-government does not exist at the regional level.

2. *Combined regional deconcentration and decentralisation.* Some functions are deconcentrated to the regional level (as in model 1), but some others are decentralised, i.e. regional authorities have the general authority to perform these functions. These could be, for example, water management, public roads, development planning, promotion of economic development etc. Decentralised functions are performed by regional public enterprise. The voivod can combine two functions: the governmental representative and the chief of such an enterprise.

---

7   See Kulesza 1991.

3. *Regional decentralisation, with regional self-government.* The region is equipped with legal entity. The regional council is elected in public elections. The voivod can be elected by the regional council or can be appointed by the prime minister.

4. *Autonomous regions with their own parliaments* (empowered to issue legal acts) and own governments and able to perform their own policies. This model would lead to full *regionalisation* of the country and, in further perspective, to its federalisation.

All these models are theoretically possible, though not all of them represent equal qualities. The third model (self-governmental region) could be recommended, although it would create a lot of ambiguity in the division of competencies between the local and regional levels of self-government (the situation could get even more complicated when the intermediate level – districts – was created). The fourth model should not be chosen as an ultimate goal of the regional reform in Poland. During the course of the reform the first model should be adopted at the beginning, then it should evolve towards the second and then, finally, the ultimate solutions of the self-governmental regions could be introduced. Moreover, particular regulations should not be introduced on the entire territory of the country, but only in those regions which would be best prepared for the reforms.

This gradual pattern of reforming the competencies of the regional authorities could – and perhaps even should – be applied in performing the new delimitation of the regional structure of Poland. It would be difficult for a single political power in this country to introduce the new regional boundaries in the form of a parliamentary bill. The new regions should therefore emerge gradually, as a result of bottom–up processes initiated by groups of present voivodships which would decide that combining their potentials would be profitable. Central authorities (the parliament and the government) should only facilitate and encourage these processes. Inter-municipal co-operation which is already beginning to develop in Poland could be one of the most important factors enhancing the emergence of new regions.

Introduction of the new self-governmental unit – the district (powiat) – will result in shifting even more tasks from central to local government.[8] It is sometimes said that this means the decentralisation of problems and difficulties the central government will be very fond of while in deep budgetary deficit. Opposite arguments state that this decentralisation will ensure greater efficiency in delivering public services and therefore more will be achieved with the same means. The final result of this reform is still to be seen, though the odds for positive outcomes seem to prevail over the dangers.

---

8   The list of new *powiats* has already been proposed and their boundaries delimited – see Jalowiecki 1993. Constant pressure of several local communities results in extending this list and creating new units, however.

For New Approaches to Regional Policies in Central Europe

It goes without saying that Poland is in a need of a modern, active regional policy. This policy should be formulated according to the following lines:[9]

For prospective regional policy

During the entire period of transformation all proposals for regional state policy have been based on *defensive assumptions*, oriented towards *reacting* to processes and phenomena that have already emerged (like unemployment or industrial decline). In practice this meant that only the so-called 'problem regions' drew the attention of those formulating state regional policies.

However, due to the acute shortage of resources these attempts have been totally unsuccessful. Moreover, there are justified opinions that concentrating on the regions which have just entered the painful process of restructuring – therefore in which negative processes prevail – leads to petrification of old regional structures and counteracts the restructuring process as such.

Any prospective approach to the processes that will take place has not been frequent enough. Thus the existing assumptions of regional policies have not been directed towards facilitating the reform of the national economy, but have been rooted in past doctrines of supporting the places facing current difficulties and problems.

It is only the phenomenon of recent days that other options of the state regional policies are being formulated. The principle of efficiency has come to be recognised and the possibility of assisting the strong regions (the 'locomotives of progress and development') has been taken into consideration. Such an attitude of regional policy could be labelled as '*prospective*' (as opposed to 'reactive' presented above), i.e. focusing on the regions which could become the nuclei of modernisation and progress in a troubled economy under transition.

For integrated regional policy

The weakness of regional policy is not a unique feature of this sector of state activities. All state economic policies have been weak during the last three years. They concentrated on narrow segments of the national economy: unemployment, social security, taxes and duties. No sectoral policy has been conducted. It is only recently that the governmental programmes have mentioned the necessity of formulating and conducting industrial, agricultural, housing, and several other state policies, though these have not been introduced as yet to a satisfactory extent.

There is an urgent need of creating an *integrated approach to sectoral and regional aspects of the national economy*. Traditionally, both systems (sectoral and territorial) used to be considered and 'planned' separately, which left regional policies weak

---

9 See Gorzelak 1993.

and ineffective, constantly losing to the preferences of the most powerful economic sectors and branches. If the Polish transformation is to be successful, this integration should become one of the main principles for any policies and actions undertaken on the Polish economic and social scenes.

There may be several suggestions for the regional aspects of the sectoral policies suitable for Poland. They should be oriented towards different goals in particular areas. The main *focus should be laid on the crucial problems of particular regions*, such as the promotion of new technologies in the greatest scientific centres, the creation of new employment in the lagging behind regions, the reconversion of obsolete industries in the old industrial regions etc. *It has to become obvious to all decision-makers in this country that no sectoral policy can be conducted without its regional aspects – and vice versa – any regional policy should be filled with concrete economic and social content.*

For internationally oriented regional policies

The geography of Europe is changing fast. The position of particular countries in this continental division of labour has ceased to be stable, as it was after World War II. The position of Poland has been changed dramatically, too, as discussed in this report. There are several aspects to this issue:

1. Traditionally, Poland was conceived as being located on the two important *European axes*: east–west and north–south. The role of these two axes has to be re-examined, as does the competitive position of Poland on both of them. It could be supposed that the reunification of Germany put Poland in a less competitive situation on the north–south axis, since more traffic in this direction would be going through the new German eastern lander, already better incorporated into Western Europe than Poland. On the contrary, the potential role of Poland as the transitory area between the West and the new East seems to be growing. If these suppositions are correct, the regional policy should reorient itself according to these lines. Poland should try not to lose competition as a transit east–west country with other central European countries, which is already becoming the case.

2. As already mentioned, only a few locations in Poland could be labelled as having a *favourable environment for foreign investment*. These regions should be strongly supported by regional policy, since (serious) foreign capital would locate there – or nowhere. This should be coupled with strong incentives for foreign capital operating in selected branches and sectors, such as high-tech industries. It should also be followed by state incentives for training and educational activities, since the quality of the labour force is known as an important location factor.

3. The deep changes in all the countries neighbouring Poland call for dramatic new methods of co-operation between the border regions. The western part of Poland has already been penetrated by the German capital, but the southern and eastern regions still seem not to have taken all their chances

of international co-operation. The role of the state regional policy is to facilitate this co-operation by developing border crossings, improving infrastructure and introducing incentives for joint undertakings.

The 'Euroregion' initiatives should be further stimulated and supported. These initiatives can become one of the best ways of opening the country to its neighbours and developing mutually beneficial trans-border co-operation. These initiatives should however, be, monitored by the government from the point of view of their role for the whole country. Monitoring should be strictly pragmatic and all ideological issues should be excluded from the overall evaluation of the already existing and emerging Euroregions with involvement in Polish regions.

For efficiency-oriented regional policy

We have to come back to the old dilemma: *equity versus efficiency*. This choice has to be re-examined in the context of the dramatic challenges of the country's economic future. The dilemma: *which regions should be assisted by the state – the strong or the weak?* is not an artificial question. It also does not seem to be an obsolete question in Poland, though the answer in favour of the weak had been provided in the West long ago. But Poland – and other east Central European countries – are in a markedly different situation. Regional policies must be congruent with the general course of reforms, in which, at least in Poland, the *efficiency* principle should play the crucial role.[10]

There are not too many examples of purely 'efficiency-oriented' regional policies in Western countries. In fact, none of the strong regions is directly supported. Instead, the Western states focus their attention on the regions needing assistance and help. The same applies to the regional policies of the Commission of the European Communities.

There are some doubts whether the efficiency-oriented regional policy would not result in too great regional differences. A simple simulation calculus demonstrates that this would not be the case, at least in Poland. At present, the relation of regional product per inhabitant between the highest and the lowest values equals 1 to 2.5. If the leaders of Polish transformations grow at the pace of 8 per cent yearly and the regions already now lagging behind at the pace of only 2 per cent yearly, by the year 2010 this ratio would grow to 1 to 5 (it has to be kept in mind that

---

10 The theses of the 3rd informal meeting of OECD Ministers responsible for regional policies, Vienna, 13 April 1994, have not yet been included in the official thinking of the Polish governmental agencies responsible for regional policies. There is no doubt, however, that some elements of the 'efficiency orientation', strongly presented in this document, will also infiltrate Poland and other post-socialist countries of Central Europe.

this is the relation of the two extreme regions: the best and the worst). In fact, the discrepancy of 1:5 is not greater than the relations existing nowadays in such countries as Italy or Spain (one should remember that in Poland there are 49 regions and in Spain only 17 and in Italy 22). It can be therefore seen that even great differences in rate of regional growth the regional discrepancies in Poland would not exceed the present level observed in some member states of the European Union. It cannot be denied that this type of regional policy would result in faster overall growth of the national economy and thus it would facilitate increase of the regional income in the lagging regions in a more distant future (e.g. in 15 to 20 years from now).

The state may support the strong regions indirectly by creating favourable conditions for the industries which 'naturally' locate in such places. These are the strong regions which take care of themselves, conducting their own development policies and competing on the world investment markets. But if this is to be fulfilled, the regions must be capable of conducting own development policies, they must constitute an economic entity being able to shape their own ways and methods of development. That is why the reform of the territorial organisation of the country should be introduced and should result in creating some 10 to 14 strong regional units.

Obviously, the state should also be responsible – through direct financing or indirect influencing private investment – for major infrastructural projects, like the motorways, pipelines, energy transmission, railways. Only the networks of major, international importance for the country should be left in the responsibility of national governments, while all other projects should be managed by regional authorities.

For regionally targeted regional policies

As already stated in this report, there are several regions in Central Europe which are on the edge of social, economic and environmental catastrophe (and in some respects this catastrophe has already taken place). Few of them have strategic importance for the entire national economies and may also have direct impact on national politics.

These regions cannot be left to themselves. The state must take its responsibility for introducing, encouraging institutionally, politically and financially the programmes of regional reconstruction.

Upper Silesia is the first on the Polish list. The complexity of its social, economic and environmental problems (to which ethnic and cultural should also be added) far exceeds the potential of this region itself to solve them. Lódz, South-Eastern and South-Western corners of the country are the next candidates for direct state intervention. The Borsod region in Hungary, Moravia in the Czech

Republic, eastern parts of Slovakia pose similar problems, although of lesser magnitude and complexity than Upper Silesia.

There should be no opposition between the efficiency orientation of regional policy and direct involvement of the state in some regions. Several of the regions mentioned above demonstrate high developmental potential which is deeply shadowed by the negative consequences of the general systemic change which took place in all post-socialist countries. It may be easily argued, on the basis of evidence collected in this report, that assisting these regions in their industrial and environmental reconversion efforts may effectively stimulate their potential which has been – or will be – covered by the avalanche of collapsing industries, unemployment, social deprivation, pollution.

However, it has to be very strongly stated that any external intervention would be completely inefficient if the regions themselves are not able to mobilise all of their social, economic and intellectual resources for self-restructuring. Global experience demonstrates very clearly that 'pumping' money from above to non-responding regions leads to complete waste of public resources and should be strongly avoided.

This message has not yet reached the consciousness of both several regional communities and national politicians in the post-socialist countries. On very many occasions one can meet in these countries clear examples of very traditional, top-down oriented approaches to the interplay between the state and the regions: the state is considered to bear entire responsibility of the fate of the regions and the regions limit their activities to claiming more and more resources from the capital of the country. The case of Polish Upper Silesia – but also of other Central European regions that need deep restructuring – show that the regional policy based on refraining from any local action and relying only on the principle '*the squeaking wheel gets the grease*' will lead to aggravation of current problems in the very near future.

State intervention should assume the form of long-ranging infrastructural programmes with focus on changing the qualifications structures of the labour force and improving the environment. However, if serious reforms of the regional structures are performed, several of the tasks now assigned to central authorities could be further decentralised and the national governments would be able to concentrate on shaping conditions for strategic problems of regional development.

The new regions will be able to create their own institutions which would supplement the state policies targeted to the problem regions. These institutions will be particularly active in training and retraining activities and in creating favourable economic environment for new investments and developments. International cooperation of regions will be further decentralised.

The final choices of the type of regional policy and the new territorial organisation of the country will be of purely political nature – but the obvious fact that the regional policy is a part of politics has to be finally acknowledged.

This choice will also have its direct impact on the regional structure of Poland – and of other Central European countries – in the coming years. Not all regions will be the winners, but those which will be able to take full advantage of new conditions will support all the post-socialist countries in their efforts to transform themselves into modern states, fully integrated with Europe.

References

Central Planing Office (1994a) *Raport o Polityce Regionalnej Panstwa (Report on the Regional Policy of the State)*. Central Planing Office, March.

Central Planing Office (1994b) *Zasady Polityki Regionalnej Panstwa (Principles of the Regional Policy of the State)*. Central Planing Office, April.

Gorzelak, G. (1993) 'Dilemmas of Polish regional policies during transition.' In G. Gorzelak and A. Kuklinski (eds) *Dilemmas of Regional Policies in Eastern and Central Europe, vol. 8*. Warsaw: EUROREG.

Gorzelak, G., Kuklinski, A., Jalowiecki, B. and Zienkowski, L. (1994) 'Eastern and Central Europe 2000 – Final Report.' *Studies 2*. DGXII of the European Commission, Luxembourg.

Jalowiecki, B. (ed) (1992) *Spoleczenstwo i Gospodarka w Polsce Lokalnej (Society and Economy in Local Poland)*. Warsaw: EUROREG.

Jalowiecki, B. (ed) (1993) *Projekt podzialu terytorialnego kraju na powiaty (The Proposal of Delimiting the Powiats)*. Warsaw: Office of the Council of Ministers.

Kulesza, M. (1991) 'W sprawie reformy terytorialnej (Concerning the territorial reform).' *Samorzad Terytorialny 7–8*.

Langota, W. and Walen, A. (1992) Agencje rozwoju regionalnego w Polsce (Regional development agencies in Poland). In J.P. Gieorgica and G. Gorzelak (eds) *Gmina – Przedsiebiorczosc – Promocja (Municipality – Entrepreneurship – Promotion)*, EUROREG, vol. 7(40), Warsaw.

Michalak, J. (1992) 'Zwiazki miedzygminne w Polsce' (Inter-municipal Associations in Poland). *Wspólnota 39*.

Wysocka, E. and Kozinski, J. (1993) 'Regionalizacja Polski – przestrzenne aspekty strategii rozwoju (Regionalisation of Poland – spatial aspects of the development strategy).' *Samorzad Terytorialny 6*.

Subject Index

References in italic indicate figures or tables.

academic centres 68–9, *69*
  Poland 66–8, *67*
age structure, Poland 54, *55*
agencies, regional development 135–6
agriculture, 10, 17, 19, 28, 40
  eastern Poland 125, *126*
  north and western Poland 126
  privatisation 24, *25, 26*, 76
  regional GDP *59*, 60
airports 102, 105
'amber route' 35
apartment cost comparisons, Poland 53–4, *54*, 55, *55*
Austrian border areas 90, 93, 94
autonomous region proposals 142

banks, Poland 99
Berlin 94, 129
Bialowieza National Park 107–8
Bialystok 95–6
bi-professionals 125–6
'big city' type of education 65
'boomerang, Central European' 127, *128*, 129
border regions 42, 93–8, 144–5
  eastern 93, 95–8, 129
  western 90, 93–5
border crossings 42, 102–3
boundary shifts 36–8
Bratislava 50, 58, 68, 76
Budapest 45, 50, 57
  airport 105–6
  foreign capital 91, *92*, 92
  labour market 65, 68, 75
budget deficits 10, *11*
Bulgaria 1–2

capital cities 45, 57–8, 68
  see also Bratislava; Budapest; Prague; Warsaw
capital privatisation 23, *25*, 83, *84*
cargo transport 101
CEC (Commission of the European Communities) 2
'Central European boomerang' 127, *128*, 129

Central Industrial District 38–9
Central Planning Office (CPO) 131
central-western Poland, potential for transformation 125
coal mining, Upper Silesia 123–4
Commission of the European Communities (CEC) 2
'Common Programme of Privatisation' 24
communications sector, privatisation 24, *25*
communist system, transition from 32–3
companies, Poland's largest 98–101, *100*
'company towns' 71, 125
  Starachowice 71, 80–2
construction projects, foreign financed 88–9
construction sector, privatisation 24, 25, *25, 26*, 26
copper basin, Legnica 106
Council of Ministers Office 131, 133
Czech Republic 1, 146
  border areas 93, 94, 97
  economic reform 6, 10, *11*
  educational level of labour force 65, 68
  demography 50–1, 52
  foreign investment and trade 13, *15, 16*, 90–1, *91*
  GDP levels *5, 7, 9*, 10
  growth forecasts 32
  industrial production 9
  international factors 36–8
  natural environment 109, *109, 111*, 112
  potential 127, *128*
  privatisation *26*
  structural change 18–19, *18, 19*
  territorial organisation 44–6, *44*
  transport 105
  unemployment 29, *30*, 73, *74*, 74, 75

decentralisation proposals 141–2
deconcentration proposals 141–2
demography 49–58, *48, 49, 54, 55, 56*
Department of Physical and Long-Term Planning 131
'depopulating regions' problem 51
distance education schools 70
'distance to capital sources' dimension 120, *121*

'diversification of structure' dimension 120, *121*
domestic trade, privatisation 26, *26, 85*
Dzialdowo, restructuring case study 80

East Slovak Range 110
east–west divisions 38, 41
east–west transport routes 35, 105, 144
'Eastern and Central Europe 2000' project 2
eastern border areas 93, 95–8, 129
eastern Poland, potential for transformation 125
Eastern restructuring, Western compared 32–3
economic categories, Poland 7, *7*
economic spatial patterns 38–42
economic power, regional 98–101, *100*
economic reforms 5–34, *5, 7, 8, 9, 11*
  foreign investment and trade 10–16, *12, 14, 15, 16*
  labour market 27–9, *27, 28, 30*
  post-Fordism v. post-Communism 32–3
  privatisation 22–7, *25, 26, 26*
  social costs 29–31, *31*
  structural changes 17–21, *17, 18, 19, 20, 21, 22*
economic restructuring *see* restructuring
educational level of labour force 63–70, *64, 66, 67, 69*
efficiency-oriented regional policy 145–6
electoral behaviour, Poland 113–14, *114, 115*, 116
employment 18–19, *18, 19*, 21, *22*, 27–9, *27, 28*
  government policy 133–4
  regional patterns 60–3, *61, 62, 63*
  see also unemployment
enterprises, Poland's biggest 98–101, *100*
environmental protection *see* natural environment
ethnic spatial patterns 42–3
European Community, GDP levels compared *5*
European reservoirs of unspoiled environment 130

Euroregions 94–5, 98, 145
exploitation of border regions 95
exports, Poland 13, *15*

foreign investment and trade
    10–16, *12, 14*
  between Central European
      countries 105
  encouraging 144
  exports 13, *15*
  foreign debt 10, *11,* 16, *16*
  regional patterns 86–98, *87, 89,*
      91, 92
foundations for regional
    restructuring 135
frontier shifts 36–8

Gdansk voivodship 35, 65, 121,
    129
GDP levels *7, 9,* 10
  EC compared *5*
  private sector share 26, *26*
  regional 58–60, *58, 59*
  sectoral 17–18, *17*
geographical location factors *see*
    border areas; transportation
German border areas 36, *37,* 90,
    93, 94–5
Germany, capital investment
    90–1, 93, 94–5
government policies, lack of
    131–5
grants, state budget 134
growth forecasts 31–2

heavy industry regions,
    restructuring problems 75
higher education centres 65–7,
    66, 67
history of Polish spatial patterns
    35–46, *36, 37*
  economic patterns 38–42
  social, ethnic and political
      patterns 42–3
  territorial organisation 44–6, *44*
housing 8, 31, 53–6, *54, 56*
Hungary 1, 146
  border areas 93, 94, 95, 96–7,
      98
  demography 50, 51, 52
  economic reform 6, 10, *11*
  educational level of labour force
      65, 68
  foreign investment and trade
      13, *15, 16,* 91–2, *91*
  GDP levels *5, 7, 9,* 10

growth forecasts 32
industrial production 9
international factors 36, 38
natural environment *109,* 111,
    112
potential 127, *128,* 129
privatisation *26*
structural change 18–19, *18, 19*
territorial organisation 44–6, *44*
transport 105
unemployment 29, *30,* 73, *74,*
    74, 75

income differentiation 29–31, *31*
industrial backwardness 41
industrial production, Poland 8, *8*
  historical development 38, 39,
      40, 41
industrial restructuring 19–21,
    20, 21, 22
  privatisation *25, 25, 26*
  regional patterns 77–9, *77, 78*
industrial type of education 65
inflation 10, *11*
integrated regional policy 143–4
inter-municipal associations
    138–9
'internal colonisation' 75–6
international factors
  Polish spatial patterns 35–8, *37*
  regional patterns 86–98, *87, 89,*
      91, 92
internationally oriented regional
    policies 144–5

Karpatia Euroregion 98
Katowice voivodship 50, 123,
    136
  big firms 99
  education level of labour force
      64–5, 68
Kosice 76, 127
Koszalin voivodship 133
Krakow voivodship 65, 121, 127
Krynki commune, privatisation
    example 86

labour market 27–9, *27, 28, 30,*
    60–76
  educational level 63–70, *64, 66,*
      67, 69
  see also employment;
      unemployment
labour productivity differences
    78–9, *78*
land price comparisons 89, *89*

leaders of transformation 47, 127
LEDA (Local Employment
    Development Action) 2
Legnica-Glogów Copper Basin
    106
'letter L' areas, Poland 40, 59, 88,
    99, 125
life expectancy 57
liquidation, privatisation by 23,
    24, *25*
local business communities 137
Local Employment Development
    Action (LEDA) 2
local elections 117
local government 136–9
location factors *see* border areas;
    transportation
Lodz voivodship 38, 51, 65, 146
  government policies 132, 133,
      135
  potential for transformation
      122–3, 127–9
  unemployment 71, 72–3
Lomianki commune, privatisation
    example 85–6
Lomza voivodship 125
'L1' and 'L2' type privatisation
    23, 24, *25*
Lower Silesia 35
Lubawka, restructuring case study
    79–80
Lublin 95

Maiopolska 35
mass privatisation 22–3
micro-regions 126–7, 130
migration patterns 51–3, 56–7
Ministry of Environment and
    Natural Resources 133
Ministry of Finance 131, 132,
    134
Ministry of Labour and Social
    Policy 133, 134
Ministry of Physical Planning and
    Construction 131, 132–3
minorities, Polish 42
municipalities, Polish 45, 140

national parks 107–8, 112
national regional policies 131–6
natural environment 41, 106–13,
    107, 108, 109, 110
  government policies 134–5
  regional potential 125, 126,
      130

north eastern Poland, potential
for transformation 125
North Moravia 75
north–south transport routes 35,
105, 144
Northern Bohemia 109
northern Poland, potential for
transformation 126

Odra River Euroregion 94
'old industrial areas' 41, 122–4
Olsztyn voivodship 125, 133
Ostrava-Kariná region 75
Ostroleka voivodship 125

parliamentary elections, Poland
113, *114, 115*
'participation ratio' 56
passenger transport 102
periphery
of Central Europe 129
of Europe 38
Poland, 1–2
biggest companies 98–101, *100*
border areas 93–4, 95–8
demography 50, 51–2, 53
economic categories 7, *7*
economic reforms 3, 6, 10, *11*
economic restructuring *76,*
77–83, *77, 78*
educational level of labour force
63–70, *64, 66, 67, 69*
employment 60–3, *61, 62, 63*
foreign capital 10–13, *12, 14,*
86–98, *87, 89, 91, 92*
foreign trade 13, *15, 16*
GDP levels *5, 7, 9,* 10
growth forecasts 32
history of spatial patterns
35–46, *36, 37, 44*
industrial restructuring 19–21,
20, 21, 22
labour market 27–9, *27, 28, 30*
natural environment 106–13,
107, 108, 109, 110
political profiles of regions
113–17, *114, 115*
privatisation, 22–7, *25, 26,*
83–6, *84*
regional policies 131–48, *141*
regional potential 119–31, *121,*
122
regional product 58–60, *58, 59*
structural changes 17–19, *17,*
18, 19
transport 101–6, *103, 104*

unemployment 70–6, *72, 73, 74*
polarisation effect 47, 119
policies *see* regional policies
political profiles, Polish regions
113–17, *114, 115*
political spatial patterns 42–3
pollution 106–11, *108, 109,* 135
population patterns *see*
demography
post-Communist v. post-Fordist
transition 32–3
power, regional economic
98–101, *100*
powiat (district) 140, 142
Poznan voivodship 65, 121, 129
Prague 57, 65, 68, 75, 127
airport 105–6
foreign capital 91, *92*
population 50, 57
price comparisons, Poland
apartments 53–4, *54*
private sector 16, 79, 99
employment 28, 60, 62–3, *63,*
76
privatisation 6, 22–7, *25, 26,* 137
regional patterns 83–6, *84*
prospective regional policy 143
provinces, Poland *36*
'proximity to capital sources'
dimension 120, *121*

rail transport 101, 102
'regained territories' 43
regional councils 135
regional development agencies
135–6
regional GDP 58–60, *58, 59*
regional patterns 3, 47–118
demography 49–58, *48, 49, 54,*
55, 56
economic power 98–101, *100*
economic restructuring *76,*
77–83, *77, 78*
foreign capital and new
international setting 86–98,
87, 89, 91, 92
labour market 60–76, *61, 62,*
63, 64, 66, 67, 69, 72, 73, 74
natural environment 106–13,
107, 108, 109, 110
political profiles 113–17, *114,*
115
privatisation 83–6, *84*
regional product 58–60, *58, 59*
transport links with Europe
101–6, *103, 104*
regional policies 4, 43, 131–48

lack of national 131–5
local government 136–9
new approaches 143–8
territorial reform 139–42, *141*
regional potential 119–31, *121,*
122, 128
'Regional, Socio-Economic
Development...' project 2
regionally targeted regional
policies 146–7
rent comparisons, Polish
apartments 55, *55*
research and development sector
employment 67–8
restructuring 17–19, *17, 18, 19*
industrial 19–21, *20, 21, 22,*
77–9, *77, 78*
regional patterns 77–83
retraining institutions 70
'River Nysa' Euroregion 94
road transport 101, 102, 103,
103, 104
Rumania 1–2
rural type of education 65
rural–urban electoral behaviour
113–14, 116
rural–urban migration *see*
urbanisation
Rzeszów 95–6

scientific employment 67–8, *67*
sectoral policies 133–4
secondary education 65
self-government 43, 45
reform proposals 140, 142, 143
sex structure, regional 51
shock therapy, Polish economic
change 6, 131, 132
Silesia *see* Upper Silesia
Slovakia 1, 147
border areas 93, 95, 96–7, 98
demography 50–1, 52–3
economic reform 6, 10, *11*
educational level of labour force
65, 68
foreign investment and trade
12, 13, *15, 16,* 90–1, *91*
GDP levels *5, 7, 9, 9,* 10
industrial production 9
international factors 36, 38
natural environment 109–10,
109, 111, 112
potential 127, *128*
privatisation *26*
structural change 18–19, *18, 19*
territorial organisation 44–5, *44*

unemployment 29, *30*, 73, *74*,
   75–6
Slupsk voivodship 133
social costs of economic reform
   29–31, *31*
social spatial patterns 42–3
'socialist industrialisation' 39, 40
'socio-economic development'
   dimension 120, *121*
south eastern Poland, potential
   for transformation 125–6
south–north transport routes 35,
   105, 144
Soviet Republics, former 1–2, *7*,
   93
spatial patterns 2–3, *4*, 44–6, *44*
   Polish history 35–46, *36, 37, 44*
   reform 139–42, *141*
Starachowice 71, 80–2
state intervention 147
   lack of 131–5
state subsidies 132, 139
stock exchange, Polish 23, 24
'Stolpe Plan' 94
Strathclyde, University of 2
structural changes *see* restructuring
subsidies, state 132, 139
Suwalki voivodship 125, 133
Szczecin 93, 121, 129

Tarnobrzeg voivodship 115
territorial organisation *4*, 44–6, *44*
   reform 139–42, *141*
tourist areas 125, 126, 130
'Tourist Six' municipalities 82–3
traditional regional division,
   Poland 35, *36*, 41
training institutions 70
transport 41, 101–6, *103, 104*
transport corridors, Poland 103,
   103
typology of regions 3, 120–9, *121*

Ukraine border areas 97–8
unemployment 10, *11*, 27–9, *30*,
   32
   and education 69–70
   government policies 133–4
   regional differences 70–6, *72,
   73, 74*, 125, 126
university-level education 65–70,
   66, 67, 69
Upper Nitra River Valley 110
Upper Silesia 38, 52, 68, 146
   pollution 106
   population 50, 51, 52

potential 122, 123–4
urban centres, foreign-financed 90
urban–rural electoral behaviour
   113–14, 116
urbanisation *49*, 50–1
   Poland 38, 39, 83

Visegrad Group 1–2
vocational training 65
voivodships *4*
   reform proposals 140–2, *141*

Walbrzych region 51, 71, 83,
   122–3
   state interventions 132, 133,
   135
Warsaw 35, 45, 51, 57–8, 65,
   127
   airport 102, 105–6
   big companies 99
   foreign capital 88–9, 91, *92,* 92
   labour market 65, 67, 68, 70
   population 50, 51
   potential 121
west–east divisions 38, 41
west–east transport routes 35,
   105, 144
western border areas 90, 93–5
Western Galicia 43
western Polish regions, potential
   for transformation 126
Western restructuring, Eastern
   compared 32–3
Wielkopolska region 35, 42–3,
   125, 137
World War II 36
Wroclaw 65, 121

Author Index

Berger, K. 108
Biuletyn Statystnczny (Statistical
   Bulletin) 21
Central Planning Office 87, 101,
   131
Central Statistical Office 25, 73
Chmiel, J. 20
Dziemianowicz, W. 13, 92
Fazekas, K. 33
Galazka, A. 89
Gazeta Wyborcza 54, 56
Gieorgica, J.P. 82
Gorzelak, G., 2, 6, 10, 11, 15,
   16, 18, 19, 33, 33, 44, 82,
   110, 121,
128, 143
Jalowiecki, B. 67, 82, 137, 142
Kornai, J. 70
Kozinski, J. 141
Kudrycka, I. 31
Kulesza, M. 141
Kyloh, R. 75
Langota, W. 135
Lehoczki, A. 106
Maddox, B. 107
Marczewski, K., 15
Michalak, J. 138
Mync, A. 12, 89
Nesporova, A. 75
Piskozub, A. 37
Polish Agency for Foreign
   Investment 12, 87
Robinson, A. 71
Rocznik Statystynski (Statistical
   Yearbook) 17, 22, 25, 26, 28,
   64
Rzeczpospolita 9, 12, 14
Spyrka, J. 106, 109
Statistical Bulletin (Biuletyn
   Statystynczny) 21
Statistical Yearbook (*Rocznik
   Statystynski*) 17, 22, 25, 26,
   28, 64
Szul, R. 89
Walen, A. 135
Winiarski, B. 93
Wprost 101
Wysocka, E. 141
Zarycki, T., 114, 115
Zienkowski, L. 58, 59
Zylicz, T. 106, 109